RESTORING

Prairie, Woods, and Pond

HOW A SMALL TRAIL CAN MAKE A BIG DIFFERENCE

Laurie Lawlor

books for a better earth™

holiday house • new york

A **Books for a Better Earth**™ Title

The Books for a Better Earth™ collection is designed to inspire young people to become active, knowledgeable participants in caring for the planet they live on. Focusing on solutions to climate change challenges, the collection looks at how scientists, activists, and young leaders are working to safeguard Earth's future.

For Jean Weedman

To put it as simply as possible, a path is a way
of making sense of the world.

—Robert Moor, *On Trails: An Exploration*

HOLIDAY HOUSE is registered in the U.S. Patent and Trademark Office.
Printed and bound in December 2022 at C&C Offset, Shenzhen, China.
This book was printed on FSC®-certified text paper.
www.holidayhouse.com
First Edition
1 3 5 7 9 10 8 6 4 2

Library of Congress Cataloging-in-Publication Data

Names: Lawlor, Laurie, author.
Title: Restoring prairie, woods, and pond : how a small trail can make a big difference / Laurie Lawlor.
Description: First edition. | New York : Holiday House, [2023] | Includes bibliographical references and index. | Audience: Ages 10-14 | Audience: Grades 4-6 | Summary: "A small rural Wisconsin community restores publicly-owned land that has become a dumping ground into a nature trail joining an elementary school and the public library and crossing three distinct ecosystems"-Provided by publisher.
Identifiers: LCCN 2022016980 | ISBN 9780823451654 (hardcover)
Subjects: LCSH: Nature conservation-Wisconsin-Juvenile literature. Nature trails-Wisconsin-Juvenile literature. | Restoration ecology-Wisconsin-Juvenile literature.
Classification: LCC QH76.5.W6 L39 2023 | DDC 333.7209775-dc23/eng/20220831
LC record available at https://lccn.loc.gov/2022016980

ISBN: 978-0-8234-5165-4 (hardcover)

CONTENTS

INTRODUCTION v

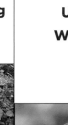

Ruby-throated hummingbird sips from cardinal flower.

Students of all ages helped
with the first prairie planting.

INTRODUCTION

This is the story of how a trail through a restored piece of land in a small, rural southeastern Wisconsin community is helping children, their families, and neighbors explore an important question: What is our responsibility to care for the world in which we live?

A trail can create unexpected connections. Not only does the Eagle Nature Trail serve as a pathway between the local elementary school and the public library, it helps connect artists and citizen scientists, readers and explorers, students and their peers as an outdoor classroom. The trail is also connecting young and old to new ways of thinking about where they live. What types of native plants can help maintain a healthy environment? Who were the people who resided in this place long ago? What animals and plants lived here?

The work of restoration and maintenance of the trail and its unique environment—prairie, woodland, and an ephemeral pond—has been an odyssey that began in 2009 and continues today. Volunteers of different ages, backgrounds, and political outlooks have banded together with only a bare-bones budget. This community-wide project has an ambitious mission: to encourage young and old alike to get outside and experience nature.

Times have been tough for the village of Eagle, population 2,014, and the Palmyra-Eagle Area School District, which includes children from Eagle and the smaller neighboring community of Palmyra. In 2019, the district, including the 152-student elementary school, was nearly closed because of funding problems and a school choice initiative.

Then COVID-19 hit.

Like schools everywhere during the pandemic, the Palmyra-Eagle Area School District has struggled to keep going. The Eagle Nature Trail has become a kind of refuge. As one Eagle teacher explained, "Nature is a powerful healing tool, if we look for it."

To deal with health and economic uncertainties while at the same time striving to change a climate-challenged world, it's more critical than ever to encourage young and old to observe deeply and make connections with the outdoors, whether it's a yard or a city park. Experiencing wonder where we live can help inspire us to save the planet. "When we see land as a community to which we belong," wrote Aldo Leopold (1887–1948), author and conservationist, "we may begin to use it with love and respect."

1

WHERE THE SIDEWALK ENDS: THE TRAIL'S BEGINNING

Not long ago, if you wanted to take the most direct shortcut between Eagle Elementary and Alice Baker Memorial Library in Eagle, Wisconsin, you had to bushwhack through wilderness. No trail led through the tangled bushes and dense thickets of trees. In the small, rural village in southeastern Wisconsin, nobody was sure what was inside the overgrown eight-acre lot. Kids claimed the place was filled with every kind of danger: prickers, poison ivy, hornets, and poisonous snakes. Grown-ups warned, "There's nothing in there. Keep out."

In autumn 2009, the future changed for this mysterious wasteland. Volunteers decided to do something about the safety of students traveling by bike or on foot between the school and the library. No sidewalk lined School Road, which could be busy during certain times of the day and dangerous in icy winter conditions. Why not cut a trail through the overgrown lot that was owned by the village and school district? Once the trees were cleared, this place would be a perfect soccer field. A playground, someone else suggested. What about a garden with donated plants from people's yards?

No one knew how much any of these plans might cost. Money has always been tight in Eagle. Founded in the mid-nineteenth century as a small farming community, the village now includes a few outlying suburban-style subdivisions. There are families who have lived in the area for generations. Not only students' parents but their

Fragrant violets carpet the woodland's edge.

Brush and buckthorn created impassable wilderness.

grandparents may have attended Eagle Elementary. Blue-collar and middle-class residents make up the population. Yet poverty is not unknown here. One in four students at the elementary school receive free or reduced-price lunches.

The Pathways Project, as the library board's new plan was initially called, would need volunteer muscle and donations of materials and services. Dave Traver, a library board member who helped spearhead the project, focused on safety and economics when he went to the village for the project's approval. "If the board would let us use the land, we'd clean it up. They wouldn't have to pay anything," said Traver, an attorney who moved from Illinois to 50 acres in the Eagle area with his wife. They later adopted two daughters who attended Eagle Elementary.

Before the first snowfall, Jean Weedman, a retired high school teacher and native-plant enthusiast on the Pathways Project committee, set off on a solo scouting mission to see what grew in the abandoned lot. Dense stands of buckthorn stood like thorny barriers. Ranging in size from squat shrubs to 20-foot-tall trees, this tough invasive species holds its leaves longer in the fall than native trees. Buckthorn had nearly smothered the remaining natives—wild cherry, cottonwood, mulberry, and silver maple—keeping them in shade for most of the year.

Weedman shoved through the thickets. Just when she was about to give up, she made a surprising discovery: a single but spectacular purple coneflower plant and several scattered hoary vervains with pencil-thin flowers. These native plants might be proof that tallgrass prairie once thrived there. Then along the edge of the trees, another surprise: two woodland natives, thimbleweed with its distinctive thimble-shaped seed heads turning cottony, and the unmistakable deep purple clusters of black elderberries.

With renewed enthusiasm, she reported what she'd found. "Nobody on the committee expected that."

In mid-March 2010, she returned to do a more complete plant inventory with Jerry Ziegler, The Nature Conservancy's land steward for southeastern Wisconsin. He had 25 years of experience working on Wisconsin restoration projects.

A landscape overgrown with so many invasive species can be almost "a dead zone," said Ziegler. When buckthorn blocks sunlight at mid-level and higher, native plants struggle to stay alive. Buckthorn leaf litter is especially tasty to non-native earthworms originally from East Asia. "Jumping worms," as they're called, gobble buckthorn litter, creating bare space on the ground—perfect conditions for buckthorn seedlings to flourish. Because chemicals in buckthorn leaves have a nasty taste, animals and insects refuse to browse on them. This invasive can seem almost unstoppable.

Windblown box elder trees had created more problems. Although these trees are a native species in the maple family, they sprawled at 20-degree angles throughout the woodland, looking like tired students slumped at their desks. The trees blocked sunlight coming through the canopy, making it even harder for native sprouts on the forest floor to grow.

Without diverse native plants for food, shelter, and places to lay their eggs, helpful insects and other pollinators had vanished. In turn, native birds disappeared. Each connecting part in the web of life had been affected.

One of the first restoration jobs on the trail was collecting and clearing garbage.

Tiny tree frog with a big voice heralds spring and hope.

Sadly, people had used the land as a dumping ground for years. Rolls of rusty chain-link fencing were coiled among scattered bike parts and broken plastic toys, tires, a legless table, shattered bottles, and cans.

Weedman and Ziegler were making their way around the litter when they heard something astonishing.

Frog song.

"The noise," Weedman remembered, "was a wonderful surprise."

They hurried across soggy ground that smelled of marshy ooze and water. In a clearing ahead was a patch of glittering water—a rare form of wetland called an ephemeral pond. Ephemeral ponds serve as important homes in spring for young frogs, salamanders, and nearly microscopic crustaceans called fairy shrimp.

Without a connection to a spring or a stream, these ponds depend on snowmelt and rain. Because the ponds dry up in summer, they can't support fish. Without hungry fish, fast-breeding amphibians have a chance that their eggs will grow into tadpoles.

"Frogs are always a good sign of a healthy wetland," said Ziegler.

On their hike back, Weedman found more woodland wonders: emerging Solomon's seal and the first unfolding heart-shaped leaves of blue and white violets.

The forgotten wilderness wasn't a dead zone after all.

Ziegler's "forensic" ecology research with soil charts, photos, and maps revealed that this piece of land had once been part of a vast tallgrass prairie with nearby oak openings or savannas with widely spaced trees. The ephemeral pond with its surrounding wetland was a remarkable bonus. With three ecosystems side by side, the hidden wilderness was revealed to be a hidden treasure.

Was it possible to restore the prairie, woodland, and pond to their former health, beauty, and diversity?

"There's always hope," said Ziegler. "I knew the ecological history of the area and was confident that native plants lying dormant in the woodland understory could come back with help from humans."

A new possible direction opened up for the Pathways Project. A trail through three natural areas would showcase Wisconsin's environmental heritage and reveal how some animals depend on all three—pond, woodland, and prairie—for food, habitat, and places to raise their young.

Weedman crafted a new mission statement: "to create a learning place for kids and adults." She was convinced that the project could be a spectacular opportunity to use native plants in the landscape.

Some committee members balked. The restoration idea sounded complicated and difficult. Where were they going to find enough individuals with the know-how and energy to do so much work?

Traver realized the project would have to reach out to a broad group of people with different skills who could work together. He believed that it was important to find a common goal. "You have to listen and find out what people need," said Traver, who has a sociable manner and quiet sense of humor. "Everyone has an individual talent that can lend itself to an effort like this. You find out what that talent is, and you develop a relationship."

To explain further, he used the example of meeting someone in the community who really loves race cars. "You start talking about engines," said Traver, the proud owner of a tractor and a dump truck. "Then you find out this fellow knows a lot about mechanics. You have that in common. He knows how to drive a tractor, fix a tractor. So you have this commonality. And you ask him if he'll come and help with the trail

Discovery of woodland violets proved a welcome surprise.

project. He does. Not because he loves nature, but because he has a skill he can use as part of the effort."

Traver is convinced you can't go at people with a frontal attack about nature. That's not how opinions are changed. There are people out there, he says, who are extremely decent. "They may not be especially appreciative of nature stuff, but there's something they can offer."

Little by little, a growing network of people willing to roll up their sleeves became involved. They included volunteer firefighters, retired teachers, a store manager, a librarian, an oil company executive, a construction business owner, a retired telecommunication engineer, a police chief, farmers, village board members, bank branch managers, principals, an educational psychology professor, an accountant, Boy Scout and Girl Scout troops, National Honor Society students from Palmyra-Eagle High School, and AmeriCorps volunteers, among many others.

Volunteers went to work collecting trash. Kids showed up to help move smaller branches and pull invasives. People appeared with backhoes, stump-pullers, more tractors, shovels, and rakes. Unexpected challenges sometimes meant adapting with new solutions. When a number of trees were cut inadvertently, the prairie area was expanded with a new design. In spring 2010, a volunteer landscape architect sketched a plan for the project now called the Eagle Nature Trail. In the summer and into the fall of 2010, the prairie was cleared of brush and weeds; the ground was leveled.

The path was laid out and crushed stone was spread. By the time the new school year began in 2010, kids could hike and ride bikes through what had once been impassable territory. Back and forth, kids walked and pedaled. Soon people of all ages from the neighborhood were stopping to watch the arrival of noisy trucks and excavators. They asked what was happening. Could they help, too?

Home Depot gave a $7,000 grant for materials, from boards to nails. On a wintry day in November 2010, a volunteer team of trained employees showed up to build an amphitheater, a boardwalk across the wetland to the pond, and a circular bench beneath a large silver maple. They worked from morning until late afternoon in the midst of snow and sleet. Agrecol, a wholesale native plant nursery and seed company, donated an acre of prairie seed mix. In spring and summer of 2011, the prairie was planted by hand. The first native oak trees were put into the ground.

Installation of crushed stones created a welcoming pathway for walkers and bicyclists. Trained Home Depot crew donated their time and skills to build the trail's boardwalk, seating areas, and amphitheater.

There's something enormously hopeful about this kind of restoration work. Nobody was sure what would happen. Would anything grow? Two summers in a row were a test. Drought gripped the area in 2011 and 2012. Volunteers struggled to keep new plants alive with buckets and long hoses. Eventually they decided to let nature take its course, said Weedman. And sure enough, in 2013, when conditions were right, the drought-resistant prairie seeds sprouted. The prairie was enhanced further with additional seeds provided by a 2013 Seeds for Education Grant from the Wild Ones organization.

Early in spring 2013, another amazing surprise emerged: a thick blue bed of fragrant violets filled the woodland. What had long been hidden was at last beginning to flourish.

In spring 2017, a near disaster rocked the project. After record spring rains in the area, the pond flooded parts of the trail and prairie for nearly a month. The water rearranged some of the new plantings, and a few prairie plants drowned.

Children emerged from school and looked with amazement at their new "lake." So many frogs leapt and called to one another, the noise was nearly deafening. Frogs were "leaping and jumping," recalled Maria Hinners, former youth services librarian at Alice Baker Memorial Library. "Some of the frogs were even trying to get through the door into the library!"

The Eagle Nature Trail has made connections with a network of local, state, and national organizations. In 2014, the trail received the Virginia M. Kline Award for Excellence in Community-Based Restoration, a program of the Aldo Leopold Foundation administered by the Friends of the Arboretum at University of Wisconsin—Madison. Named a Certified Wildlife Habitat in the National Wildlife Federation's worldwide network of mini-refuges, the Eagle Nature Trail has also been recognized officially as a monarch waystation by the Wild for Monarchs Campaign, a joint project between Wild Ones and Monarch Watch to help conserve migrating butterflies. With assistance from the Million Trees Project of the Living Lands and Waters organization, 25 oak trees were planted at the trail in 2019. On Earth Day in 2020, 2021, and 2022, 110 red, bur, and swamp white oak seedlings were distributed to student families with instructions for planting in their yards.

Dedicated teachers continue to find new and creative ways to bring the

Sandhill cranes, once endangered, have made a dramatic comeback to the area—thanks to the kind of environmentally friendly practices used on the trail.

curriculum outdoors. "You see the difference it makes when kids go outside and experience the environment directly," said Matt Stich, former Eagle teacher and principal. "They're not just looking out a car window at nature or looking at a TV or computer screen."

Each year the quality and diversity of habitat and wildlife continues to improve—with special appearances by creatures as wide-ranging as foxes, possums, ground-hogs, rabbits, woodpeckers, hummingbirds, owls, hawks, migrating sandhill cranes, and deer. Plenty of opportunities to pitch in and help are available seasonally for kids and grown-ups. In 2021, a new woodland pathway was cleared and connected to the main trail.

"Sometimes restoration work seems like a long, slow slog," said Weedman. "Other times I look back and I think about what we've done and how we've managed to stay close to our original mission. I always feel encouraged when I see young kids arrive on the trail and get excited about nature and then come back later in high school or college to volunteer. We never know whose attitudes about the environment we've helped change."

2

TRAVELING BACK IN TIME TO UNDERSTAND WHAT SHAPED THE LAND

To understand what shaped the land where the Eagle Nature Trail is located today, imagine a camera that hovers 9,974 feet in the air and does not move. (That's as high as a bald eagle can soar above the clouds.) Imagine the camera's powerful lens focusing nonstop on the future spot of the Eagle Nature Trail on the ground below. And now imagine this amazing eagle-eye camera taking a photograph every year for 25,000 years. (A very long time!) What might be discovered?

If all 25,000 images from oldest to newest are viewed one after the other like a fast-forward film, dizzying changes unfurl. Floods rush in, dry up, then braid across the land in rivers and streams that twist and turn. Lakes and ponds appear, creep, vanish. Dark clumps of vegetation drift, then flit away like swift fish. The land seems alive.

What is happening?

Start with the first image from 25,000 years ago. There's not much to see—just glaring white as blank as a piece of paper. Why? At that time, the Eagle Nature Trail would have been buried by a mile-thick sheet of snow and ice, the slippery surface of a wind-blasted glacier.

Between 25,000 and 14,000 years ago, most of what is now known as Wisconsin was shrouded with the massive Laurentide Ice Sheet that covered millions of

Early spring morning on the trail connects young and old with the outdoors.

Native prairie coneflowers offer welcome habitat for insects of all kinds.

square miles across most of Canada and a large part of the northern United States.

How did glaciers move? Think what happens when pancake batter is poured on a hot griddle. The more batter you add, the more the pancake's edge moves outward. Massive glaciers, created from compressed snow that never melted, grew heavier year by year. The weight and force of gravity forced the edge to flow outward so that the glacier crept a few inches, or sometimes up to several miles, every year.

When temperatures warmed, the glacier began to melt. Ice slivered, cracked, exploded, and crashed. As the edges shrank, the glacier would have appeared to move backward. Everywhere there must have been the sound of water—rushing, dripping, gurgling. Sea levels rose. When temperatures cooled, water refroze. Snow fell and replenished the glacier. The glacier shoved forward again.

Glaciers did not move in massive unison. Individual lobes or sections hurry-crawled like icy fingers across the landscape, pushing and probing at different speeds. Two lobes, named the Green Bay and Lake Michigan Lobes, crashed together like a slow-moving car wreck about 16,000 to 14,000 years ago.

When the lobes melted and pulled apart, between 15,000 and 8,000 years ago, a hummocky ridge 90 miles long was created. These low hills, trending north-south like a narrow wrinkle in a blanket, are now part of the 56,000-acre Kettle Moraine State Forest. The Southern Unit is located only a few miles from the village of Eagle.

As soon as the ice vanished, plants began to migrate onto the damp, cold landscape. Carried by wind and water, the first "pioneer" seeds arrived and grew. Rough lichens came first. These tiny plants clung to rocks. As plants grew, then died, the organic material they left behind slowly turned into layers of soil. In flat terrain created by an outwash plain, the soil accumulated over thousands of years—perfect conditions for a vast prairie that would one day flourish with deep-rooted grasses and flowering plants.

Throughout what's now known as the Midwest and the Great Plains, nearly 170 million acres of prairie thrived—thanks in part to the action of those early glaciers. The vast, diverse prairie ecosystem spanned the area from Canada south to Texas, from southern Indiana west to Nebraska.

The rich grasslands soon attracted browsing animals. Herds of mastodons with curved tusks browsed on spruce and willows along streams. Woolly mammoths with domed skulls and thick, reddish coats made this place their home, along with herds of giant elk and caribou. The prairie teemed with other animals that look as if they were drawn by cartoonists: flat-headed peccaries—members of the wild boar family— and giant beavers as enormous as black bears. All are extinct now. Bison, well adapted to extreme cold, eventually grazed in huge herds. Smaller grassland creatures also made the prairie their home—everything from rodents and hares to foxes and 13-lined ground squirrels.

Dragonflies, swarming midges, and buzzing mosquitoes and flies became food for prairie birds—all manner of songbirds and grass dwellers. The first bird arrivals may have carried mollusks and tadpole snails. Soon toads, snakes, turtles, and fish thrived there.

Between 11,000 and 8,000 years ago, the first human hunters (called Paleoindians by anthropologists) roamed the land. They used spears with fluted stone points to kill game, which was sometimes driven out of hiding with purposely set grassland fires.

Indigenous peoples in this part of Wisconsin created mysterious earthen forms called effigy mounds 1,500 years ago. Varying from 5 to 6 feet in height and

20 to 1,300 feet in length, the mounds were shaped like birds, turtles, snakes, and lizard-like creatures. Often located next to water sources, the effigy mounds may have been created by a cooperative network of Indigenous peoples during what's now known as the Late Woodland Period (1,400 to 750 years ago). This was a time when new technology was being embraced and new art was being created. Bows and arrows replaced spears. Pottery was decorated with familiar pond creatures—frogs and polliwogs.

While Indigenous peoples have lived here for thousands of years, most of the early written observations about tribes weren't recorded until the seventeenth century by French missionaries and fur traders. Language barriers and prejudice often created confused accounts.

Fatal diseases and trade goods like guns and liquor introduced by Euro-American colonizers quickly created conflict and speeded change. Pushed away from the East Coast by colonists, tribal nations moved west to the Great Lakes region. Wisconsin became what's known as a "shatter zone," a place where displaced tribes fleeing distant regions moved into areas already long occupied by Indigenous peoples, creating social and cultural disruption.

One of the groups living in southeastern Wisconsin prior to 1500 were the Potawatomi, who called themselves "Keepers of the Sacred Fire." They had developed their own

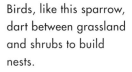

Birds, like this sparrow, dart between grassland and shrubs to build nests.

Bees are important pollinators.

systems to survive spiritually, culturally, and physically. In fall they harvested wild rice and hunted deer. In winter they hunted in small family groups. In spring they did "sugaring" in sugar-maple camps. In summer they gathered in semipermanent villages that might contain more than 100 individuals. They lived in dome-shaped wigwams made with wooden pole-and-sapling frameworks covered with hides or grass mats. Large council houses were used as places for leaders of the tribe to make decisions and hold ceremonies. One of the biggest villages in the 1820s was located on the Mukwonago River, only a few miles from what would one day be called Eagle.

In summer they grew corn, beans, a variety of squash, including pumpkins, and tobacco. They gathered wild rice, wild plums, raspberries, and various tree nuts, including hickory nuts and acorns. They used horses and birch-bark canoes, and were known to travel as far away as Iowa on hunting expeditions. In southeastern Wisconsin, other tribes included the Ottawa, Chippewa, Menominee, Ho-Chunk (Winnebago), and Sac. On occasion more than one tribe might live together in one village.

Potawatomi family stands in front of a log cabin in Wood County in northern Wisconsin around 1920. Elders have identified the woman in the center as Mrs. Frank Young. The man on the right is community leader White Pigeon.

In 1768, approximately 60,0000 Indigenous people lived in the entire Great Lakes region, which included Wisconsin. Of these, an estimated 3,000 were Potawatomi. Wars in North America between European superpowers quickly changed life for the Potawatomi and others. The War of 1812 and the Blackhawk War in the early nineteenth century unleashed catastrophes for tribes already in southeastern Wisconsin.

In 1830, the Indian Removal Act signed into law by President Andrew Jackson began what would be one of the final stages in a land grab as Euro-American settlers flooded west in ever-growing numbers. The Potawatomi and other tribes signed the Treaty of Chicago in 1833 that basically gave away more than five million acres in southeastern Wisconsin and northeastern Illinois in exchange for the promise of cash, annuity payments, and a place to live in the Missouri River Valley.

An estimated 15,000 Potawatomi and Ho-Chunk had lived in southeastern Wisconsin before Euro-American settlement. "Treaty after treaty, parcel after parcel, the Potawatomi sold off their homelands," wrote one historian. By 1829, the tribe had lost 70 percent of its original lands. Beginning in 1837, some Potawatomi were forced west to reservations in Kansas and Iowa.

Many, however, drifted north to the far reaches of Wisconsin, the Upper Peninsula of Michigan, and as far away as Canada to resist being moved westward. Without an official homeland, they struggled to hunt, fish, and practice their religion, customs, language, and traditions. The "Strolling Potawatomi," as this landless group were called, moved often to try to avoid governmental control.

By the 1870s and 1880s, Potawatomi numbers in Wisconsin had dwindled to somewhere between 175 and 280 individuals. Not until 1913 were they provided with 11,440 acres in small, unconnected 40- and 80-acre parcels in a cutover (deforested) region in northern Wisconsin.

Today the population of Potawatomi is roughly 1,400. Since 2010, 12,000 acres in Forest County have been tribally owned, supported in part by tribal casino revenue.

3

SETTLEMENT AND CHANGES TO THE LAND

Since the arrival of the first Euro-American settlers about 180 years ago, the land that would one day be home to the Eagle Nature Trail has undergone dramatic changes that occurred with such bewildering speed (in the grand scheme of the past 25,000 years) that we need special maps to help visualize what has been lost and what remains.

A survey map is a handy tool to help identify and keep track of the small, special piece of land where the Eagle Nature Trail would one day be located.

How does this kind of map work?

Begin with a perfectly square sheet of paper. Call it Waukesha County.

In real life, it's 24 miles on each side. Now, fold the paper square in half, then in half again. Keep folding a total of four times so there are 16 identical squares. These squares are called townships—6 miles on each side. The township tucked at the southwest corner is called Eagle.

Fold Eagle Township even smaller—in half, then in half, then in thirds, then in thirds again—to make 36 squares. These are called sections. Each has a number, and each is exactly one mile on each side and contains 640 acres.

Section 23 is located just about in the middle of Eagle Township.

Over the years, teams of cartographers (mapmakers), naturalists, ecologists, botanists, geographers, and geologists have tried to come up with a picture of long-ago

Lush prairies and oak openings (in distant center) once covered this area. The pictured grasslands and oaks, once extensively farmed, are being restored by relatives of Frederick Sprague, an early local settler.

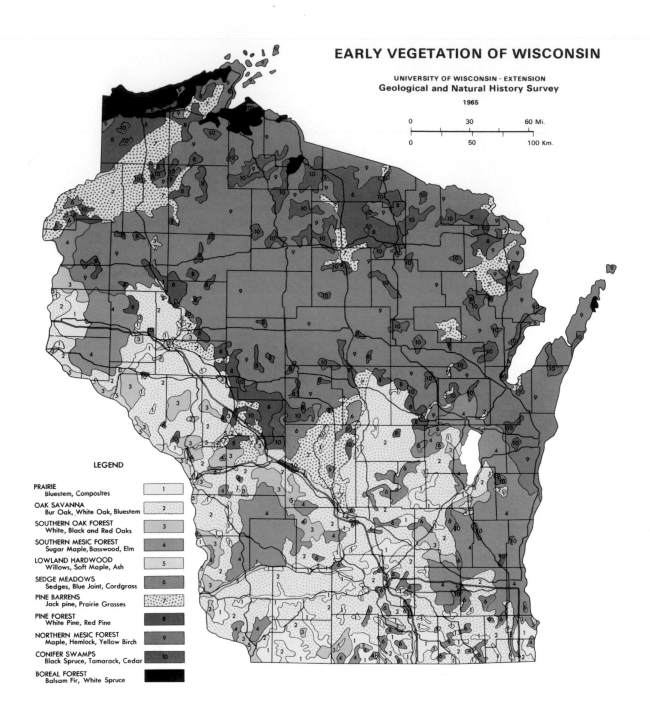

EARLY VEGETATION OF WISCONSIN

UNIVERSITY OF WISCONSIN - EXTENSION
Geological and Natural History Survey

1965

0   30   60 Mi.

0   50   100 Km.

LEGEND

PRAIRIE
Bluestem, Composites ___1___

OAK SAVANNA
Bur Oak, White Oak, Bluestem ___2___

SOUTHERN OAK FOREST
White, Black and Red Oaks ___3___

SOUTHERN MESIC FOREST
Sugar Maple, Basswood, Elm ___4___

LOWLAND HARDWOOD
Willows, Soft Maple, Ash ___5___

SEDGE MEADOWS
Sedges, Blue Joint, Cordgrass ___6___

PINE BARRENS
Jack pine, Prairie Grasses ___7___

PINE FOREST
White Pine, Red Pine ___8___

NORTHERN MESIC FOREST
Maple, Hemlock, Yellow Birch ___9___

CONIFER SWAMPS
Black Spruce, Tamarack, Cedar ___10___

BOREAL FOREST
Balsam Fir, White Spruce

Complex assembly of early surveyor records
helped create this 1965 map of Wisconsin
showing the varied vegetation that existed
prior to Euro-American settlement.

Waukesha County, Eagle Township, and Section 23. What plants flourished here? What did the landscape look like? What animals might have made this place their home?

In the 1950s, a vegetation map was created to show the ecosystems across Wisconsin before Euro-American settlers arrived in 1835. The process was complicated. By combing through early surveyor field notes—often scrawled and illegible—researchers compiled lists of plants, acre by acre.

A pattern of ecosystems began to take shape, ranging from prairies and grasslands to different kinds of forests and wetlands. Each ecosystem was mapped with a different color. Before 1835, the county was 5 percent prairie, 54 percent bur oak savanna, and 29 percent mixed forest of maple and oak.

Prairie fires pushed by fierce winds could race across the landscape day or night, faster than a horse could gallop.

Because of adequate yearly rain and snowfall and plenty of sunlight, the different ecosystems might easily have altered in time from prairie to oak savanna, from oak savanna to oak forest. Why didn't this happen?

Fire.

Bur oak trees and native plants remain after a controlled burn.

Because of lightning strikes or fires that were set on purpose by Indigenous people to flush out game, this land regularly burned. Dry grassland was perfect fuel for late-fall and early-spring fires. Fires pushed by strong wind raced across prairies, overwhelming all trees except mature bur oaks with thick, fire-resistant bark. Rivers and lakes served as barriers to stop or slow fires.

Scorching fire destroyed woody shrubs and invasive weeds. Fire did not, however, wipe out deep-rooted prairie grasses and plants—like bluestem and switchgrass, compass plant and rattlesnake master. These plants are among many species that evolved to withstand fire, drought, and extreme cold and heat. Regular visits by fire helped prairie plants come back even stronger in the spring.

Bur oak openings, or savannas, are hybrid environments in which native prairie grasses and other plants mix with woodland species. Fires that rushed through these openings removed competition from invading undergrowth while sparing mature bur oaks.

Fire was both destroyer and shaper, transformer and creator.

FIRST LANDSCAPE FIELD NOTES

On a sweltering morning on August 17, 1835, a seven-man surveying crew trudged across Eagle Township carrying chains, poles, and axes. Leading the way with a compass and a small notebook was Noah Clark Jr. The crew's job was to walk and measure each side of every section.

The work was hot and tiring. Mosquitoes and flies buzzed. Wet and muddy, the crew forded streams, slogged through marshes, clambered up hills, and scrambled through thick woods. Clark and his crew were marking boundaries to identify exact locations of land soon to be sold by the federal government to individual settlers.

The four chainmen, as they were called, carried a heavy, 66-foot chain attached to wooden poles to measure the boundaries. The men plunked the ends of the poles into the ground and stretched the chain to measure, calling out the length as they went. Following straight lines, the crew moved around the perimeter of each one-mile-square section. The axmen drove wooden stakes into the ground to mark section corners. Sometimes they cut a blaze or mark on the side of an especially prominent oak to show property lines. These were called "witness trees."

Clark sketched a map and scribbled notes about what he saw as they walked. To the north of the land that would one day be the Eagle Nature Trail, he noticed "land moderately rolling and first-rate dry prairie." Describing nearby land in another direction, he wrote, "Land west of prairie broke second rate—prairie gently below and first rate."

He kept a keen eye for "first-rate" land that could be profitably cultivated. He was not interested in the prairie's beauty or the way the grass—taller than a man—rolled like waves in the wind. Quality timber that could be cut and hauled away was also noted: "stands of oak, white oak, and yellow oak." Were streams they encountered fast or sluggish? Clark wasn't interested in the clarity of the water or the profusion of fish. He wanted to know where a water-powered mill could be located.

Sometimes he complained about "wet prairie with deep marshy places" as they sank to their boot-tops in soggy ground. In emphatic scrawl, he wrote: "Marsh unacceptable" or "trembling marsh—water too deep to raise mound [for stakes]."

The crew was supposed to follow the shoreline to measure small lakes or ponds. Sometimes they skipped that step. Maybe fierce bugs were biting. Maybe the crew was growing mutinous. The ephemeral pond in Section 23 seems to have gone completely unnoticed in Clark's rough map and notes. At that point in the summer, it was probably dried up.

Likewise, Clark does not mention seeing Indigenous people, who may have been hiding and watching the strange group of white men tramping across their ancestral homeland. There are clear indications that Clark knew that tribal nations were in the area. In the northwest and southeast corners of his rough map he sketched wobbly faint lines he labeled "Indian trails."

As a result of the surveying crew's work, the future home of the Eagle Nature Trail was given a name, a very unpoetic-sounding identification number: T5N R17E.

AXE, PLOW, AND COW

Even before the ink was dry on surveyors' maps, change raced across the region at lightning speed. The land rush began in 1839 as soon as the land office opened its doors in Milwaukee. Good land could be purchased for only $1.25 per acre. A real bargain, everyone said.

Although the Wisconsin Territory—formerly part of the Michigan Territory—would not become a state for nine more years, nearly 650,000 acres in southeastern Wisconsin were sold in 1839. By 1845, that number topped three million acres. The first wave of arrivals were New Englanders, New Yorkers, and settlers from Europe. Some made the trip by barge along the Erie Canal and then across the Great Lakes by ship. After they docked on the western shores of Lake Michigan, they pushed overland in wagons or on horseback. The population of Waukesha County skyrocketed from 2,256 in 1840 to 19,258 just 10 years later—a whopping increase of 750 percent.

Axe, plow, and cow utterly transformed the land. So many trees in southeastern Wisconsin were cut for fuel and house and fence construction that entire forests disappeared. Tree acreage in the county plummeted from 156,000 in 1836 to 59,613 in 1885. Before sowing wheat and later corn and alfalfa, farmers used steel plows to tear through rich prairie sod, turning it "wrong side up" and exposing thick roots of native plants. What had once been vast, diverse grasslands that stretched horizon to horizon were now row crops.

Marshland decreased from 18.6 percent of the county's area in 1834 to 12.4 percent two years later. Wandering livestock grazed native grasses and bur oak saplings alike—destroying oak-opening plants so quickly that no one knew what species had vanished.

Horse-drawn plows were used in the area throughout the nineteenth and early twentieth centuries. This photo was taken using a glass-plate negative around 1900–1910.

Wide-open fields reveal glimpses of the boundless horizon of the original Eagle Prairie. The village of Eagle, around 1940, appears in the middle in the far distance.

Farmworker with two-person saw stands beside remaining old-growth tree, one of many that once grew here. Wisconsin scientist Increase Lapham (1811–1875) was so alarmed by the destruction of the state's forests, he began in 1867 to write and lecture extensively on this topic.

By 1850, nearly 60 percent of the county's land had been converted to farms. Farmers planted wheat—a cash bonanza until insects destroyed the crops and soil fertility was depleted. The number of cattle in the county leapt from 5,981 in 1850 to 18,788 by 1870.

With the increase in cropland, fire was eventually suppressed—much to the relief of early farmers, who saw unpredictable fires as a terrifying force to be conquered. Gustaf Unionus, who immigrated from Sweden, settled 20 miles from Eagle in Pine Lake. He witnessed his first prairie fire in November 1841:

> The fire made us panicky. When in the evenings we saw the red glow in the sky coming closer and closer . . . [as] the flames . . . raced up tall trees. We seemed surrounded by those fiery pillars and more clearly we heard in the distance the fearful roaring like thunder. We feared that our cabin and we and our animals might soon be consumed by flames.

With fires suppressed by vigilant settlers determined to plant crops on grassland, diverse ecosystems that had thrived for thousands of years began to vanish. Dense stands of trees crowded oak openings and choked out native plants. Woody shrubs and trees invaded prairies not already converted to cropland or pasture. Oak forests not harvested for timber were scavenged by cattle and pigs that destroyed native woodland flora.

To early settlers, the prairie seemed boundless, its bounty inexhaustible.

Jonathan Parsons in 1840 purchased 160 acres that would one day include the Eagle Nature Trail. He called the place "the Prairie Farm."

Parsons's neighbor Frederick A. Sprague, who arrived around the same time, wrote: "The prairie in which I live is a complete flower garden every week and almost every day from the first of March to the first of October. . . . [S]ometimes the prairie is a beautiful blue, sometimes pink, sometimes yellow and white with flowers almost all of which are new to me."

Only a few decades later, the Parsons and Sprague children would have only half-forgotten memories of the vast grasslands, oak openings, and mixed hardwood forests.

Elderly Frederick A. Sprague, enterprising farmer and physician, poses for his portrait in scuffed boots, holding a broad-brimmed hat and cane with the head of a sharp-beaked bird. He once bragged to a relative back in Massachusetts that his sons (eventually seven in all) killed a dozen raccoons (one weighing 30 pounds) and caught 60 pounds of fish from a nearby creek in just two hours.

Wildlife, too, vanished as the land was converted to agriculture, woods were cut for lumber, and wetlands and ponds were drained or filled in for cropland. The last bison in Wisconsin was killed in 1832; the caribou, decimated by 1840; elk, gone by 1868. By 1900, beavers had been trapped into oblivion. Cougars, fishers, martens, and wolverines would vanish by the first decades of the twentieth century. The wild turkey, once abundant, was wiped out.

Across Wisconsin thundered flocks of migrating passenger pigeons—"inexhaustible," numbering in the hundreds of thousands. Naturalist and writer John Muir (1838–1914), who lived in Wisconsin as a boy, recalled the flocks flowing "like a mighty river in the sky." Their habitat destroyed, the birds were hunted to extinction. The last wild passenger pigeon in Wisconsin was shot by a hunter in 1899.

As American writer and farmer Wendell Berry would later write, "We plowed the prairies and never knew what we were doing, because we never knew what we were undoing."

4

ENVIRONMENTAL STRUGGLES IN THE TWENTIETH CENTURY: NEW TECHNOLOGY, GREED, AND NATURAL DISASTERS

The first decades of the twentieth century began what would be a critical test for the survival of healthy land in Wisconsin, the rest of the Midwest, and the southern Great Plains. High crop prices convinced many farmers to boost yields by plowing and planting every inch of their farms—"fence post to fence post." Woodlots were cut to extend fields. The last stretches of native grassland soil were lifted, broken up, and turned over. Hills once considered too steep, and valleys known to flood, were plowed into cropland.

By the time the United States entered combat during the last year of World War I (1914–1918), high demand overseas and government-guaranteed prices—$2 a bushel for wheat—encouraged even more over-plowing. The latest technology, a "one-way" disc plow that was faster and more efficient, could be pulled by a diesel-powered tractor. No one understood that the "Great Plow-up" would help create one of the worst environmental disasters yet experienced in the United States.

In 1929, the New York Stock Market crashed and what would later be called the Great Depression began. Wheat and other crop prices collapsed. People across America lost their jobs, their homes, their farms. Banks closed. Factories were

Less than five undisturbed acres of the once vast Eagle Prairie remain. Located less than a mile from Eagle Nature Trail, this precious remnant is a refuge for rare native plants like prairie dropseed, pasqueflowers, prairie smoke, and lanceleaf coreopsis. Today, growing housing development nearly surrounds the unplowed prairie.

shuttered. Federal programs did not exist to help people with no money, no food, and nowhere to live. In Wisconsin and throughout the "breadbasket" of the Midwest and the Great Plains, a terrible drought began in 1930 and lasted nearly a decade—a period marked by record-breaking heat waves, dust storms, plagues of grasshoppers, fires, and floods.

From June 1933 to May 1934, Wisconsin's precipitation was only 69 percent of normal—the lowest ever recorded. In some places in the state, annual precipitation was 12 to 15 inches below normal. Crops withered and died as soon as they began to emerge from the powder-dry soil. After a short rainfall in early April 1934, the rain did not fall again for two months.

Temperatures in early May hit 108 degrees Fahrenheit in places. Pasture grass turned bone-white and brittle. Cattle began to starve. Without living crops, the fields looked gray, parched. The most fertile topsoil—fine and light—had no roots to hold it in place when the wind blew. Anything that moved—a person, a wagon, an automobile— would leave a trail of boiling dust. Wind snatched the dirt and hurled it skyward.

On the morning of May 9, 1934, the sun rose bloodred. The wind from the west began to murmur, then howl. People in Eagle Township spotted a dark cloud on the horizon and hoped it would bring rain. No such luck. The biggest, longest dust storm headed east across the continent from the Great Plains. For the next two days and one night, the terrifying dust storm carried 300 million tons of dirt 1,500 miles. As the wind reached 60 miles per hour in Wisconsin, the swirling black blizzard blocked the sun. Noon turned to midnight from Canada to Texas.

In Eagle Township and elsewhere across Wisconsin, dust stung skin, blinded eyes, and choked anyone who ventured outdoors. Plumes of dust slashed like knives through any new corn, potato, or alfalfa plants. People covered their faces with damp rags and hid indoors with doors and windows shut. Dust slithered through the cracks.

One Wisconsin man recalled waking up and seeing the outline of his body in the bed because of grit drifting into his home all night long. Wisconsin folklore claims that pails placed beneath cows filled faster with dirt than they did with milk. When the dust storms finally let up, people came outdoors and discovered their crops were gone and their world had been turned upside down. "You should have seen the dust," one farmer later recalled. "Buried fence rows like snow."

Lung disease—called dust pneumonia—afflicted the young and the elderly. Searing heat continued through July 1936 in Wisconsin and the Midwest, with temperatures that again hit 108 degrees for days. Before the invention of air-conditioning, this killer heat wave was partially blamed for the deaths of an estimated 5,000 people across the United States.

In 1935—only 100 years after Euro-American settlement—another map was created with an ominous and somewhat desperate-sounding name: the Wisconsin Land Economic Inventory. On the heels of almost six years of drought and heat, a careful tally was made of land cover (cultivated plants, marsh, and trees) and improvements like schools, cheese factories, creameries, houses (both occupied and abandoned), and roads. Trained forestry grad students walked each 40-acre section of Waukesha County and made notes to document "the current and potential use of land . . . so that abandoned farms, cutover forests, and other idle land could be resettled, reforested or otherwise put to productive use."

On the inventory map of Eagle Township, Section 23 is cut through the middle by a gravel state highway. The land is labeled "C" for "cleared cropland." Nearby is "non tillable permanent pasture" (recommended to be replanted with forest), a few remnants of "grass marsh," and scattered oak and hickory trees. The 1935 inventory doesn't show ephemeral ponds, perhaps because the seasons had been so dry. Once again, no one thought to record the pond in Section 23. But somehow it had managed to survive.

The rest of Eagle Township was not so lucky. What had once been a vibrant patchwork of diverse ecosystems was now being labeled with categories that included "stump pasture," "dead timber," and "poor land previously cropped." The idea behind the inventory was to identify "submarginal" pieces of land—areas that were as environmentally devastated as moonscapes. With this information, the state government planned to purchase unproductive farms and encourage farmers to resettle elsewhere.

UNEXPECTED HEROES OF THE LAND

On a hot morning, July 29, 1937, the first aerial photograph of Section 23 was taken. The black-and-white image below shows a landscape that looks scarred, gouged, and pocked in places by years of drought, heat, and wind. Even though it's midsummer, a time when stands of corn can tower over a grown man, the fields are not uniformly dark with row crops.

From high overhead, it's easy to see the grid-like patchwork of farms that stretch in all directions. Inside Section 23 is a 60-acre farm shaped like a long rectangle; its short end abuts a gravel state highway that leads into the village of Eagle, population 391.

A strawberry-shaped scar in the southern third of the 60 acres reveals the outline of the ephemeral pond—now with just a white pinprick of water in the middle. Plow marks have been stitched around the pond in a neat square.

Aerial photo from summer 1937 captures the effects of drought on the land that would one day include the Eagle Nature Trail.

To reach the farmhouse, a traveler had to turn off the gravel road and head north on a dirt track flanked by another row of trees. A winding drive snakes to the house and barn with gleaming pale roofs. Nearby are a small vegetable garden and a fenced area for a cow or a few pigs. Scattered around the farmyard are hopeful shade trees that from above look like squat, dark sponges.

From this aerial photo it's not possible to see the people who live on the farm, or their clothes dancing on the laundry line near the house. It's not possible to hear chickens scratch the hard-packed ground, the chorus of crickets, or the harsh cries of crows. The photo doesn't show the black-eyed Susans—the last prairie plants to keep a precarious foothold along the railroad right-of-way. The viewer has to imagine the lonesome wail of the Chicago, Milwaukee, and St. Paul across the farm's northwest corner—so close to the house that dishes rattle on the shelves.

Like so many farms in the area during tough economic times, this place was plagued with evictions by the sheriff and foreclosures by local banks. From 1937 to 1943, four different owners tried and failed to hold on to the land. Those who didn't have the money to own their own land worked someone else's. A "cropper," or tenant farmer, who couldn't come up with rent or didn't have money for seed or equipment had to move on and start again somewhere else.

Frank Splechter was a stout ne'er-do-well cropper with a temper and a sixth-grade education who drifted with his wife and children from Kansas to Mississippi to Wisconsin doing field work and renting houses. Convinced that the grass was greener on the other side of the hill, Frank always had a plan to make more money. The problem, a relative later remembered, was that he didn't like to work.

Elizabeth, his wife, was said to be so small she could stand beneath one of his outstretched arms. Blond, with pale gray eyes, Elizabeth at age 20 had emigrated alone from what is now called Hungary. She had only 10 dollars. Her death in 1931 at age 43 affected her children deeply. Agnes, 19; her sister, Margaret, 17; and their 13-year-old brother, Frances, nicknamed Fritzy, left home as soon as they could.

Agnes and Fritzy would one day become the unlikely heroes in the story of the 60 acres in Section 23 that are now the home of the Eagle Nature Trail.

SNAPSHOT IN TIME: JULY 1941, SECTION 23, EAGLE TOWNSHIP

One of the earliest close-up photos of the land where the Eagle Nature Trail would be located was taken on what may have been a hot July afternoon in 1941. On that summer day, Agnes and her brother posed with their family in a photograph taken on the farm that Frank had "cropped" since 1936 with his second wife, Lucy. Valued at only $25, the ramshackle house, like so many that Frank rented over the years, had no indoor plumbing.

The image shows the family near a tall tree that billows and shakes in the wind. Sunshine shimmers off the nearby barn. Agnes, almost 30 and unmarried, stands thin and pensive in wire-rim glasses with her brown hair pulled back. She does not smile. Throughout her hardscrabble childhood of endless chores and constant moves, she never had a chance to play. Even in her few baby photographs, she has a somber expression. On this day she wears a cotton print dress decorated with flowers, sturdy shoes, and silk stockings that she has frugally rolled around her ankles.

Her dream after graduation from Oconomowoc High School in 1930 was to enter the convent of the Missionary Sisters. To her regret, she was not accepted into the order. Instead, she took a job working a 60-hour week in a white uniform as a no-nonsense nurse's aide at St. Mary's Hospital.

In the photo taken that day in July, Fritzy, 23, in the bottom right of the photo, grins with the confidence of a young man about to escape his moody father and dawn-to-dusk drudgery as a neighbor's ill-paid farm laborer. In only a few days he'll travel to Milwaukee to enlist in the army.

World War II had been raging in Europe since 1939. Although the United States would not officially enter the conflict until after Japan bombed Pearl Harbor on December 7, 1941, farm boys like Fritzy were already signing up for combat training. Fritzy's dream was to go overseas in uniform and prove himself a hero before the fighting ended. At 5 feet 10 inches and 165 pounds, ruddy-faced Fritzy was used to hard work.

Regular army pay must have seemed like an incredible amount of money to someone who'd been poor all his life. Fritzy planned to save his pay as a nest egg for the day he would finally be able to marry his sweetheart, a local girl.

Splechter family gathered in July 1941 for a photo on the land that would one day be the Eagle Trail. Fritzy kneels in front on the far right. His sister Agnes stands behind him.

Fritzy had been promoted to sergeant when this photo was taken, sometime before his death in 1944.

Standing in the back row in the photo is his 28-year-old sister Margaret, with her husband's arm around her shoulders as if they're sharing a secret. Their two young children, Robert, five, and Mary, three, squirm as if to run away from Frank, pictured in overalls. His hands are big, and he has a distinctive smell ("Like a pigsty," a relative said). His wife, Lucy, stands shyly in an apron. Her thin lips are pressed into a slit as if she senses something's burning in the oven.

Fritzy's life did not work out the way he'd planned. After training, he became part of the "Go Devils," the Ninth Infantry Division's Sixtieth Infantry Regiment. He was made a sergeant, saw action in Belgium and Germany, and was killed in the line of duty on October 17, 1944, during a desperate fight with German troops. The battle took place in the Huertgen Forest, a hilly area in Germany with the same kinds of small lakes as southeastern Wisconsin where Fritzy swam and fished as a boy.

Fritzy was awarded the solemn honor of the Purple Heart medal. His remains were eventually returned to a cemetery in Dousman, Wisconsin. His death was undoubtedly a sorrowful shock to Agnes and her sister.

Then a secret was revealed.

Throughout Fritzy's service overseas, he'd been quietly sending his army paychecks to Agnes for safekeeping. (Clearly, he did not trust his father with the money.) In July 1945, Agnes used Fritzy's $3,800—a sizable sum—to buy 60 acres of Section 23, the same farm that Frank and Lucy had been renting. Agnes let them continue to stay there, probably rent-free. Frank died in 1961.

Agnes kept the land in her own name. She visited but never lived on the farm. "She was not an outdoorsy person," said her great-niece Barb Ziemer, who remembered ducks on the ephemeral pond when she went there as a child. Agnes stayed busy as a nurse's aide and later as a private nurse. She often grew a small garden, depending on where she lived. She stayed in contact with her sister's children and grandchildren.

Not one to let anything go to waste, Agnes made holiday gifts of mittens knitted from the yarn of unraveled sweaters, and canned jars of pickled beets. (One batch was particularly notorious because she'd reused the brine from the previous year.)

Soon, the 60 acres and the surrounding farms began to change. Aerial photos show the rapid growth of subdivisions encroaching closer and closer to the Eagle Nature Trail's future location as the population of Eagle increased from 460 in 1950 to 620 in 1960. As the years tick past, the photos show trees that seem to grow and expand. Meanwhile the pond shrinks, blossoms, shrinks again. Little by little, cultivation ceases on the 60 acres that Agnes owned.

In March 1965, 54-year-old Agnes sold the land for $13,500—not to a corporate farmer or a real-estate developer, but to the Wisconsin Conservation Department as part of an effort by the state to acquire parcels of submarginal land to create open space and a new park, Kettle Moraine State Forest.

A May 17, 1966, aerial photo shows the beginning of rewilding. No more crops. Trees begin to invade. So do exotic shrubs from nearby subdivisions with manicured lawns. Dotted with streetlights, the subdivisions are crisscrossed with asphalt streets and gutters for stormwater runoff. Now the original house and barn on the Splechter property are gone.

June 13, 1969—another image. More undergrowth, more trees. Plants surround the pond.

In 1972, the state sold the land to the village. By September 26, 1979, a thicket of trees had almost completely taken over—the photo reveals trees so thick they touch one another. A mysterious dirt-bike path loops through the nearby field. In the remaining cropland, what can't be seen in the image is the ever-increasing presence of chemical fertilizers, herbicides, and pesticides to boost yields of corn and soybeans.

On November 14, 1985, Agnes died. Her decision to sell the land to the state of Wisconsin would have a lasting impact on the future of open space, environmental restoration, and cooperation in the community. In 1987, Eagle Elementary was built for prekindergarten through sixth grade. In 1995, the new library opened inside the village hall building.

The eight-acre lot encompassing the ephemeral pond would remain overgrown, mysterious. Waiting.

This August 1992 aerial photo reveals how many more houses, roads, and stores have encroached on open farmland. The new light-colored building for Eagle Elementary is visible.

Like a stone thrown into a pool of water, an individual's actions can create a ripple that reaches out in all directions and touches the lives of many different people.

Fritzy's tragic sacrifice as a young soldier ultimately resulted in something positive. With the money he gave Agnes for safekeeping, she bought the land that would eventually be transformed and restored. "Fritzy was the beginning. Agnes was the end," said Ziemer, who helped care for her great-aunt Agnes when she was elderly. "I think it would have made Fritzy happy to know about the Eagle Nature Trail and the children who use it. He would have been so pleased."

5

AUTUMN ON THE TRAIL

A new school year begins at Palmyra-Eagle Area Elementary. Even though the air and sunlight feel as warm as summer, the calendar says September. Restlessly, the third grade waits for the teachers' signal to line up to go outside to a special place. At last—freedom!

Across the parking lot the children leap, twirl, and trot. Some walk arm in arm, others playfully frog-march. Everyone seems to know where to go. Like a flock of wild turkeys crossing a road, they hustle to the Eagle Nature Trail sign, where they stop and wait for their teachers. "This is *our* nature trail," one of the boys proudly tells a new classmate. Like many of the other students, he's been here for many different activities in all seasons and weathers. "Just follow me."

Crickets sing. Under the children's feet rusty fallen leaves crunch and crackle. A few bees and bright monarch butterflies dart among the yellowing prairie plants—milkweed leaves gone pale, brittle coneflower blooms turned inky black and spiky as spiders.

Today is a special day on the Eagle Nature Trail: the September 11 National Day of Service and Remembrance. The children have come to inspect the growth of seven special trees grown from the seed of swamp white oaks at the National September 11 Memorial in New York City.

The trees were planted in 2013 by students representing kindergarten through sixth grade. Each of the trees is fenced and marked with plaques honoring citizens,

"Sunset by the Pond," a recent youth winner in the Eagle Nature Trail Photography Contest, celebrates the waning light of autumn. Photographer was 10 years old when she took this picture on the trail boardwalk.

Third graders gather on the trail to examine the September 11 commemorative trees.

armed forces personnel, firefighters, police, medical workers, and airline employees and passengers affected by the tragic events of September 11, 2001. The events that day have been described as the most devastating foreign attack on American soil since the attack on Pearl Harbor in 1941.

The events of 9/11 seem long ago and far away to most of the students. Some of their parents were barely teenagers when that horrific day occurred. The children agree that planting a tree is a good way to remember special people. "Trees grow more than 100 years if you take care of them and they have good soil and water," a fifth grader tells the group. "They'll be here a long time."

The swamp white oak seedlings sprouted from acorns collected by a former Eagle resident, Phil Hall. He gathered them from the specially planted collection of oaks that line the memorial in New York. Hall and the Eagle Lions Club donated the seedlings to the Eagle Nature Trail. The trees are a little bit of New York City transplanted along the trail.

When a photo is passed around showing the 2013 seedlings, the students seem surprised. "So small!" says a fourth grader. Later, she stands beside one of the eight-year-old oaks, which towers several feet above her. "See how much it grew?"

Swamp white oaks can grow more than a foot a year and reach heights of 50 to 60 feet. The children notice right away the different textures of the lobed leaves: glossy green above and white and fuzzy on the underside. These oak leaves have not changed to yellow-brown or orange-brown yet. The bark, still smooth, will eventually curl in ragged scales—the perfect homes for caterpillars, which in turn are an important source of food for many kinds of native birds. An estimated 511 species of insects depend on oaks for food and shelter. No other tree supports so much life.

All morning energetic classes from every grade explore signs of oak growth and changes in the seasons. Sumac blazes red. Wind hurls down the first leaves of the big cottonwood near the ephemeral pond. There's been no water in the pond for months, but the grass and sedges that grow within its shoreline remain green and hopeful.

Overhead four sandhill cranes soar, calling to one another as they begin to assemble for migration. The air seems filled with motion and expectation. Colder weather will arrive soon.

Blue jays shriek and dive high in the trees. Since they overwinter in the woods, they must get ready for winter. The noisy, clever birds are experts at gathering and planting acorns. Blue jays have specialized beaks with hooked, pointed ends that can rip open an acorn husk to get at the nutritious seed inside. Their expandable esophagus allows them to carry in flight an incredible load—five acorns at once. When they land, often miles away from the acorns' origin, they push each nutrient-rich seed into soft soil. Then they tap it with their beak to hide their treasure for future use when cold, hungry winter arrives.

Since oaks can't roam around to spread their acorns far and wide, blue jays have become some of the trees' most helpful partners—superb oak farmers. A single blue jay can gather and bury nearly 4,500 acorns in the fall. A jay can't remember where every acorn is buried. As a result, an estimated one-quarter of their food cache eventually sprouts into oak trees.

The web of life—the connection between oaks, birds, soil, water, and climate—includes people, too. The children seem to keenly sense this today. While standing under a silver maple to have their class photo taken, a fourth-grade girl becomes distraught. What's wrong? Another student has stepped on the stem of a fading aster. "Watch out!" the tearful girl says as she struggles to make the stem stay upright. "This is part of our family."

MILKWEED POD TOSS

No milkweed, no monarchs, the saying goes.

There's an important relationship between these native plants and monarch butterflies. The plant serves as nursery and feeding station for caterpillars that eventually become butterflies. Young caterpillars nibble milkweed, which contains a chemical that accumulates in their bodies. By the time the caterpillar transforms into a bright orange-and-black butterfly, the chemical has become so strong that it causes a reaction from any creature attempting to snag a butterfly snack. Yuck! The nasty taste convinces bird predators to stay away.

Full-grown butterflies sip nectar from sweet-smelling pink blossoms of milkweed— a high-energy food source for their coming migration. The butterflies' visits to the blossoms in turn help pollinate the milkweed. More butterflies, more milkweed. More milkweed, more butterflies.

Unfortunately, monarch butterfly populations have dropped dramatically in recent years because of habitat loss, pesticide use, and changing global weather patterns caused by climate change. In 2016, third and fourth graders started a tradition at the

Prairie monarchs abound among milkweed leaves.

Eagle Nature Trail that helps monarch butterflies and provides a fun activity as well. It's called a Milkweed Pod Toss.

Milkweed pods make handy missiles. Shaped like a crescent dinner roll, the pods contain tightly packed, small brown seeds cushioned by white fluff. When the pods are ready, they turn from soft green to brown. The students carefully pry open the pods with their thumbs. Then they cheer and throw the exploding pods as far as they can into the air over the prairie. White milkweed fluff scatters like early snow. When the seeds land, hopefully they'll begin to grow.

Milkweed has become bountiful on the prairie over the years. Not only does it benefit butterflies, it's also a boon to pollinating bees and to hummingbirds that enjoy milkweed blossoms' sweet nectar.

STORYBOOK STROLL ON THE TRAIL

The trail is designed for exploring not only nature but books as well. Groups of kindergarten and preschool children meet at the amphitheater to hear stories shared by a librarian from Alice Baker Memorial Library. Between picture books about owls, foxes, worms, and other fascinating creatures, there's lots of singing and stomping and moving of arms.

In late September, 16 signs are set up along the trail with pages from a picture book about a tree that falls in a neighborhood and what happens when the community comes together to cooperate and help one another. During two bright, clear days, 129 children and 37 adults from the school and the local community follow the trail and read each page as they walk. "It's a way to hike and read at the same time," explains Maria Hinners, youth services librarian for 20 years.

Before third graders begin the Storybook Stroll this morning, they sit in the amphitheater to talk about their own favorite trees.

"A pine!" someone shouts.

"Mine is in my backyard. I climb it."

"I sit under mine in the shade or when it rains."

"My favorite is an apple tree."

"I don't know what mine is called."

Running, hurling, and laughing with friends are part of the fun of the Milkweed Pod Toss, which also encourages important new growth on the prairie.

Following the stroll, this group is going to be the first to explore a new trail cleared with volunteer help from University of Wisconsin–Milwaukee students and others. The edges of the trail have been marked with logs to keep hikers from stepping on the woodland violets. Laid in a line, the logs are tempting balance beams.

"This way!"

The group winds through the woods that were once so densely packed with thickets of buckthorn that no one knew a towering 100-year-old silver maple was hiding there. The new trail circles the maple. Its multiple trunks seem to reach the sky.

"Look up!" someone shouts. For a moment, nobody speaks. They gaze at the leaves dancing in the wind.

Farther along the trail the group discovers a fallen 50-foot cherry tree. "Just like the book we read!" someone says.

They climb along the trunk covered with rough and peeling bark that reminds one girl of "very brown potato chips." Hidden among the muddy, upturned roots is a mysterious hole. Who's in there? A few students crouch and look inside, waiting. When nothing pokes a head out, they hurry away.

This dead tree is a perfect shelter in winter for possums and raccoons that hide in burrows. Salamanders also overwinter in this kind of refuge. Hibernating garter snakes curl deep underground. The most numerous inhabitants are hard to see: microscopic bacteria, species of fungi, and thousands of insects that break down dead trees to help recycle nutrients in the soil.

When it's time to head back to class, a boy lingers near the fallen tree. He finds two branches to make into an *X* on the ground. "So someone will come along and know this is a treasure spot," he says. "Somebody's home."

OBSERVING THE TRAIL WITH A CAMERA

To inspire people from the community and school to visit the Eagle Nature Trail, a photo contest for all ages has been held every year since 2015. All the photos are of critters, plants, and scenes of the woods, prairie, and pond. "It's a way to show the incredible variety of what's along the trail," says Alli Chase, the library director.

Each fall there's a reception, and awards are given—including a People's Choice Award by folks from the community who vote for their favorites. Forty photos were entered in the 2021 contest, including seven from photographers under age 18. The images on display include everything from a wise tree frog perched on top of a coneflower blossom, and a close-up of a deer so well concealed that its ear looks like a leaf, to resting hummingbirds and a swarm of black-and-red beetles.

A teenage girl, who was given a camera by her grandparents for her birthday, is thrilled to have her photo on display. Her whole family—including her three-week-old brother—have gathered to view the photo exhibit.

6

WINTER WONDERS ON THE TRAIL

Winter weather in Wisconsin is never predictable. Sometimes the snow falls and drifts higher than kindergartners' waists. Sometimes the snow doesn't fall for weeks, and fifth graders can play soccer out on the frozen field near the school's playground. What is predictable is that winter drains light from the sky early. The sun seems to barely skim over the tops of trees and roofs before it disappears again. Even though days are shorter this time of year, there is still action on the Eagle Nature Trail.

Because the trail isn't plowed, students can practice being arctic explorers on their journeys to the library. When the way is clear enough, kindergarteners from Eagle Elementary put on their boots, hats, and coats and wander along the trail to Story Hour at the library. "The first thing I always ask them when they come in the door," says Maria Hinners, youth services librarian, "is what did you see out on the trail? What did you hear? What did you smell? They know I'm going to ask them, so they're quick to tell me."

This is the time of year when the children notice how they can see their breath wreathe like smoke, and the shattering sounds boots make when they jump on ice. Being able to go outdoors for fresh air helps brighten the grayness of some afternoons.

Freezing and melting snow and ice helped shape the landscape for
the trail and the region.

Leaping on the path shakes free winter doldrums.

Matt Stich, former principal and fourth-grade teacher at Eagle Elementary, has witnessed firsthand how the trail connects the school and the library, a place where kids can go at the end of the day. "The trail is a bridge between the two institutions of knowledge. Sometimes older siblings take younger brothers and sisters on the trail to the library. They assume a leadership role and give tours to siblings along the way."

Children are good at noticing what's changing during different seasons, explains art teacher Beth Dobberstein. "There's always something new to observe with all five senses." If the weather's mild enough, the students bring sketchbooks or an iPad to record images. "We talk a lot about looking closely. What do we see down low? Up high? Close by? Or in the far distance? I'm always reminding them to look deep and then look deeper."

"Kids are always excited to be outdoors. It's a chance to move around and explore," she continues. "Being outside, seeing the open sky, feeling the breeze affects mood. It can help create hope."

Just as in other schools across the country, COVID-19 and quarantines have posed challenges for students and teachers. The Eagle Nature Trail has taken on a new significance, Dobberstein says. "I think it's important to be safe and yet be able to say to a classroom of students, 'Let's go enjoy being outdoors together.' Looking for changes around us on the trail is a way to help kids process their emotions, too. They get a sense of change, but also of stability."

Art and science came together in 2020 in a third-grade project that spanned outdoor and indoor activities. Tammy Mueller, a classroom teacher, and Dobberstein collaborated on the extended look at native plants, how they grow, what their cells look like. A Go Outside grant from the Wisconsin Department of Natural Resources helped fund the project.

Third graders undertook a multi-season project that began with planting 200 native plants—everything from lavender hyssop, joe-pye weed, and blue lobelia to cardinal flower and meadow blazing star. The kids kept careful watch on the plants as they grew. Later, they sketched and painted the plants. Using microscopes in the classroom, the students examined slides of plant cells and a living plant. They made clay models of the cells they observed under the microscope. During the colder months of late fall, the kids displayed their paintings and clay models in an all-school exhibit.

"The main emotion when kids go outside is excitement," says Mueller, who has taught at Eagle since 1992. "I think that the trail provides lots of learning opportunities for kids to experience hands-on science. We have the trail right in our own backyard."

When a heavy snow falls, as it did in February 2021, the drifts are so high on the Eagle Nature Trail that it's hard for even grown-ups to walk. Cold wind stings. Breath

Knee-high drifts make trail trekking an arctic adventure. Students now check out something new at Alice Baker Memorial Library—snowshoes!

fogs glasses. It's a foolish time of year to travel anywhere without a hat and mittens.

Everywhere along the trail are stories of the hunter and the hunted, pursuit and escape. Tiny tracks of field mice crisscross crooked prints of leaping rabbits. In winter it's possible to sense how many different animals live here from the prints they leave behind.

On the pond, the wind shoves snow into ridges that look like wave patterns in the sand on a beach. What's happening to the frogs in the midst of so much cold? How do they manage to survive this long, cold wait for spring to return?

In fall, spring peepers crawl beneath leaf litter and logs in the woodland to hibernate. Their bodies produce high levels of glucose, which acts as a natural antifreeze and also keeps the tiny frogs—only 1½ inches in length—from dehydrating. The frog's cells are protected from damage even as its body freezes solid—a kind of living frog-cicle. It's a remarkable adaptation.

Even though it's a cold February dusk, a deep duet of great horned owls echoes nearby. These owls are among the earliest birds to build nests and lay eggs. Measuring nearly two feet tall, with piercing yellow eyes and tufted feather "ears," these tawny owls can fearlessly attack skunks and porcupines—perhaps that's why they've been nicknamed "flying tigers." The nature trail has plenty of small rodents for their dinners.

One expert on winter hikes is Marlin P. Johnson, a faculty member at the University of Wisconsin–Milwaukee for many years. He serves as resident manager of the University of Wisconsin–Milwaukee at Waukesha Field Station. Under his leadership, this preserve has been restored to support communities of plants and animals native to Wisconsin. Johnson led a group of winter hikers of all ages on the Eagle Nature Trail in 2011.

Here is his list of cold-weather-friendly activities and science experiments that are fun to do:

1. *Snow can be a protective blanket. Take a thermometer. Put it in the snow. If you compare the temperatures above and below the snow, what do you discover? If it's warmer under the snow, who do you think might live there?*

2. *Use a magnifying glass to discover insects that you didn't know*

lived in the snow. Tiny snow fleas, also called springtails, are active under the snow. As soon as there's a bit of warmth and sunlight, they crawl up on top of the snow to breed. They look like black bits of pepper that dance.

3. Watch the shadow of a tree grow. Keep a journal to watch how the shadow changes as the day progresses. The shadow starts on one side, very long and lean. At noon, the shadow turns short. At the end of the day, the shadow grows long again.

4. Take a hike with snowshoes—or just good boots. After your journey, make a picture and map of your trip. What did you see?

5. Build a snow person.

6. Make a snow angel.

7. Create a decoration using a pine cone covered with peanut butter and rolled in birdseed. Hang it from a tree.

8. Listen to the silence.

9. Record the animal tracks you discover. Write a story about what the footprints reveal.

10. Make tea from sprigs of white cedar. White cedar has soft, feathery foliage and scale-like flat leaves. Sometimes it's called arborvitae. Go outside and gather four sprigs of white cedar. Fill a medium pot with six cups of water and bring it to a boil. Once the water comes to a boil, lay the cedar on top. Let the water boil for at least 10 minutes. Once the water is tinted green, remove it from the heat. Add honey if you like. Drink and enjoy.

Identifying northern white cedar (arborvitae)
Leaves: dull green, flat fan-like sprays
Bark: stringy, shreddy, reddish to gray

White cedar was used by early settlers to build homes and piers because the wood is extremely rot-resistant. This is the same wood that's used for shingles and fence posts.

7

SPRING SURPRISES ON THE TRAIL

Wind shifts in the high bare branches of the woods. March air smells faintly of damp earth and new growth even though there are still patches of ice on the trail. Dry prairie stalks rattle. Soggy snow piles shrink on the pond. Nearby comes a startling sound as faint as paper ripping: the first yearning song of a wood frog.

Without fish predators, the ephemeral pond has become frog heaven. Lacking any permanent inflowing or outflowing stream, the pond depends totally on plentiful snowmelt and rain. There's not much time before the sun will begin to evaporate the water. In these early, cool days before hungry snakes, salamanders, and bullfrogs wake up and start searching for tadpole snacks, the wood frog has a head start to attract a mate, breed, and lay eggs in the water. One cluster contains about a thousand eggs. Before the eggs hatch, however, the wood frog will have already skedaddled into the woods again.

Soon, other frogs take turns singing to attract mates on the ephemeral pond. Each frog has its own distinctive tune: the high, flute-like love song of the awakened spring peeper; the scratchy creaking of a chorus frog; the low purr of a pickerel frog. Any tadpoles that emerge from eggs are in a race against time. They have to grow fast and become big enough to avoid being gulped by other pond inhabitants.

During the heavy rains of 2017, when the pond flooded and lapped up into the prairie, frog song was nearly deafening. That spring, the frog population exploded. New visitors showed up, including a pair of mallard ducks that nested on the shore.

Buds seem to emerge overnight in the woodland.

A rainy April night is the perfect time to spot a shy, elusive salamander that's 7 to 13 inches long. After a quick earthworm meal, tiger salamanders crawl out of burrows under tree stumps and rocks and dash down to the pond to lay eggs. They are black with uneven yellow spots that look as if they were painted by a distracted artist. The prehistoric-looking, slimy-skinned creatures have short, stout legs, broad heads, small eyes, and round snouts. Once they reach the pond, they lay up to 100 eggs that cling in a large round mass to floating twigs. After only 40 days, the eggs hatch into larvae. Undaunted by the risky life in a shrinking pond, salamander larvae, which look like tadpoles, have a clever backup plan. They can hide underground and overwinter. This gives these carnivorous little creatures an edge next year when spring comes again.

After laying eggs, the adult salamanders quickly retreat to safer hiding spots in the woods. Adult salamanders have unusual talents that seem almost unbelievable. Like swallowing their food with help from their eyeballs. Salamander eyeballs look like Halloween gags. The eyeballs are hard, and their eye sockets extend into their mouths. Why? When a salamander gulps a meal of cricket, the salamander's eyeballs sink into the sockets to help squash the food and force it down its throat.

Do not try this trick at home.

Restless children can't wait to get outside and explore. When a group of second graders is asked what are the first things they want to do outdoors and why, they answer:

"Watch leaves come out."

"See flowers bloom."

"Look for deer running. Maybe a fox."

"Going outside makes me happy."

"And excited."

"The fresh air helps me a lot. I get energy. I don't feel trapped like I do indoors."

Song of green frog beckons from the pond as soon as the temperature begins to warm.

First joyful journey for kindergartners looking for signs of spring.

THE POWER OF PRAIRIE FIRE

Even though it's still early spring, work has begun on the trail. For the first time in six years, the prairie is undergoing a prescribed (controlled) burn. On a bright March morning in 2021, a crew of nine volunteers and trained fire workers in boots and special face masks assemble.

Everyone knows their job. Some carry water tanks. Others tote drip torches, cylinders filled with a flammable liquid that drips from a wick once it's lit. Turned upside down, the torch drops bits of fire on the dried grass. Other folks carry "flappers," poles with a rubber piece on one end that's used to swat and smother escaping flames.

The wind is not too strong, not too light. And the dead grass on the prairie isn't too wet. A controlled fire in the dried vegetation will help renew prairie plant growth and eliminate invasives. Accomplishing this burn early in the spring means that insects will have a chance to replenish their populations and be available for nesting birds migrating into the area.

A natural fire break has been created by the gravel trail on one side. The fire is

In only a few days, tender sprouts emerge from the ash.

carefully set at one end with a drip torch. The flames are pushed gently by the wind across the prairie. When the fire hits a stand of dried bluestem, flames shoot up with a roar. The fire crawls, explodes, smolders, reignites, and crawls along. Volunteers move along the edge, keeping careful track of where dried grass burns, making sure it's out completely after the flames pass. Everywhere smoke lingers.

It's possible to imagine the fires when this was part of Eagle Prairie more than 200 years ago. Only fire can keep this restored prairie healthy.

When students come out to visit a few days later, they stand nervously beside the blackened, ashy field and ask what happened. They seem reassured when they hear how prairie flowering and seed production will be even more bountiful later this spring. "If we can just be patient," says trail volunteer Karen Akroff, "in a few weeks the prairie will begin to be lush again."

A few days pass. First graders on their way to the library pause on the trail to examine small, green blades of grass poking up from the charred prairie. This seems like a hopeful sign. They are eager to share ideas about what people can do to help the environment.

"Pick up trash."

"Recycle cans if you see one on the ground."

"Plant trees."

"Water plants."

"If you see a baby bird that's fallen from a nest, put it back."

CELEBRATING EARTH DAY

A brown thrasher calls from the trees that are already beginning to bud. Sparrows, robins, cardinals sing wildly. In early April, especially before a rain, the sweet smell of violets fills the trail. Across the woods a bed of blossoms has spread like a brilliant blue-and-white carpet.

To celebrate Earth Day, a group of third graders hurry down the trail with clipboards, paper, pencils, and magnifying glasses. This is their first springtime trip to the trail. They rocket in all directions, first to the pond, then to the prairie, and into the woods. They're here to write poetry. First, they have to find just the right place to write. Some immediately plop down in the grass and begin. Others use their magnifying glasses to look carefully at emerging buds and bits of milkweed fluff. Others hike deeper into the woods to find a perfect subject.

"I found Peter Rabbit's house!" a girl calls from the woods, where she's discovered a mysterious hole.

"Bones! I found bones," another boy announces.

Being outside inspires this sampling of poetry:

Spring

Green leaves are on trees.
Beautiful birds are chirping.
I smell fresh green grass!
  —Kaylee L.

Blooming Flowers

Little blooming buds
Flowers blooming in the Spring
Bees getting pollen.
  —Ella T.

Deer

I hear and see deer.

They are walking in the woods.
They can make loud sounds.
     —Ashton D.

When it's time to leave, the third graders exuberantly shout, "Happy Earth Day!"

On a sunny, warm day, a second- and third-grade combination class gathers at the amphitheater on the trail to share similes and poetry inspired by Earth Day. This group went into the woods earlier in spring. On Earth Day they returned to the same place to write about what they saw.

"Drawing helps me notice. See?" says one girl, holding up her picture. "I'm trying to show when there was almost nothing. Now everything is blooming again."

"I listen to different sounds," explains a boy. "That gives me ideas."

The ants were as happy as people
Seeing a unicorn for the first time.
     —Aubrey

Outdoor sounds, sights, and smells inspire spring poetry.

Birds are like seeds.
When they're in the sky
They drop down to the ground.
   —Gabby

Green beetle
Shines like sun
Crawls like daddy longlegs.
   —Matthew

Purple petals hiding in their den.
Spiders and beetles hiding in their home
And getting ready to go back before rain.
We're the giants of the city.
We're bigger than them and they're all scared.
   —Jackson

OWLET RESCUE

It's a windy day in April 2021. The pair of great horned owls that were calling to each other in January and February have made a nest in the top of a 35-foot-tall pine just outside the library. Like many owls, this pair is not good at building nests. They may have taken over this nest from a sloppy crow or perhaps a slapdash squirrel family.

For weeks, the well-camouflaged pair has been using the Eagle Nature Trail prairie and woods to hunt for food for their two owlets that hatched in early March. Observers on the trail have noticed owl pellets at the base of several trees in the woods. A pellet is regurgitated bits of bones, teeth, and fur that owls can't digest. The pellet looks like a small, dark nugget.

Although the owlets are just fledglings and still don't know how to fly, they practice daredevil tricks on the edge of the nest—just like human siblings sometimes do. Suddenly, a gust of wind knocks one owlet from the nest. It falls unhurt to the ground. While the owl parents scream and swoop, the dazed owlet sits on the ground until a passerby strolls closer. This Eagle resident decides to return the owlet to the nest. He straps on a bow-hunter's climbing belt and puts on special boots. With the owlet tucked inside his shirt, he makes the journey up the tree, and returns the frisky baby to its family.

The next day, owlet overboard again!

This time Matthew Wilhelm, park ranger with the Wisconsin Department of Natural Resources (DNR), gets a call from the Eagle police department to help with the rescue.

Wilhelm takes the owlet in a cardboard box to the local animal rehab organization to make sure it's all right. Before its X-rays, the owlet raises all its tough-guy feathers so that it looks as big and as fierce as possible. No broken bones. After examining a recent pellet, the technician gives the owlet a clean bill of health. "Clearly his mom and dad were taking care of him. He had been eating plenty of mice and rabbits," says Wilhelm as he prepares for the owlet's return to his family.

To avoid any more jumping hijinks, a new nest must be created. How? Wilhelm's wife, Lisa, a DNR master naturalist, suggests that a basket of some kind might work as a nest replacement. The only kind of basket Wilhelm can find is a white plastic laundry basket. Not very attractive, but practical.

Owlets settle into their new, sturdier nest—complete with comfy blanket.

Wilhelm drills holes in the basket, finds some strong rope, and climbs the fire department's longest extension ladder. He manages to securely tie the basket to the tree with the rope—just below the original nest. He adds a few homey touches: an old blanket and some sticks.

While the owl parents swoop and make threatening shrieks, Wilhelm, wearing leather gloves, carefully removes the uncooperative second owlet from the nest. He shifts this little creature into the laundry basket, then returns for the adventuresome owlet in the cardboard box.

Climbing all the way up the ladder holding a squirmy creature the size of a pineapple with

The fire truck's extension ladder is the only way to reach the nest atop the tall pine.

razor-sharp talons doesn't seem like a good idea. Wilhelm tucks the owlet inside a messenger bag, hoists it carefully over his shoulder, and makes the second climb. The transfer is a success. Two weeks later, the owlets are fine, having adjusted to their new, sturdy nest.

Meanwhile, the library's owl family have become celebrities. People from the village gaze at the growing birds with binoculars. "Takes owls to bring the community together," says one resident after Wilhelm gives a Zoom presentation describing the rescue.

"This was a group effort," says Wilhelm. "I couldn't have done it without the police department, the fire department, and so many others who helped."

8
SUMMER SPLENDOR ON THE TRAIL

Nothing happens slowly as summer approaches. Every day seems to reveal a new blossom, birdcall, insect buzz, or bellow from the prairie, woodland, and pond. Overhead, swallows fly loop the loop. Everywhere you can sense the clamor and flash of bluebirds, swallows, orioles, and red-winged blackbirds, calling to one another, building nests, feeding their young. Three birdhouses along the prairie edge are fully occupied. A "No Vacancy" sign should be posted outside.

June is a perfect time for restless children to go outside and do something energetic and important on the Eagle Nature Trail. There's much to be accomplished before school officially ends.

Summer reveals abundance on the prairie. Big bluestem begins to tower over the children. Growing as tall as nine feet, "turkey foot," as it's sometimes called, grows in clumps with roots that can reach moisture 10 feet deep. Soon the grass will turn from steely gray-blue to red, brown, and purple. Waving in the wind are stands of vigorous, three-foot switchgrass that will turn bright yellow later in the fall. Tall, graceful Indian grass, another drought-resistant plant with deep roots, shines golden brown as it bends.

Mixed among these shimmering grasses are compass plant with emerging bright yellow flowers, prickly rattlesnake master, black-eyed Susans, purple

Prairie plants explode with color and height by midsummer—just in time for Fourth of July.

coneflowers, and the elegant blue blossoms of spiderwort. With dozens blooming at a time and flowers lasting for two to four weeks, there is always a wonderful variety on display. Some flowers move on to seed production while other new species are starting to reveal blossoms. By "taking turns," the prairie plants reduce competition. Each plant gets its time and place in the sun. That's also why the prairie provides an almost continuous source of nectar for different insect pollinators.

It's not surprising that one cubic foot of prairie soil contains much that is not easily seen—nearly half a million nematodes. Nematodes are tiny, non-segmented worms that are 1/500 of an inch in diameter and 1/20 of an inch in length. While there are thousands of different species, they all help in some way to recycle nutrients in the soil. Some consume bacteria and fungi. Most are not plant pests, but rather help control disease. Even though they are hard to see, nematodes are an essential part of the soil food web. Without healthy soil, prairies, woods, and wetlands cannot thrive.

Soon, school will officially end for the year. Heat shimmers. Above the wetland plants of the ephemeral pond, dragonflies soar. Birds swerve and swoop. Early one morning a shy deer peeks between the trees as if checking for water. It's

Fawn is an early visitor to the pond.

Cabbage butterflies

Fourth-grade "weed warriors" set off with bags to gather invasives.

hard to believe that only months earlier, this place was as cold and barren as the Arctic.

Before the last day of school, every class will come to the trail to help pull invasives called garlic mustard and dame's rocket. The students arrive full of energy, eager to be "weed warriors." Some of them have done this work before. For others, removing invasive plants is something new.

Jean Weedman explains what to look for and how to carefully pull the weeds, smack the roots on the ground to knock off the dirt (the students' favorite step), then bend the invasives and stuff them into black garbage bags. Garlic mustard has a definite smell. "Like garlic pizza," says one boy. Because the garlic mustard blossoms are gone, it will be more challenging today to find and pull this fast-growing plant that overwhelms forests and crowds out native species. One garlic mustard seed head can contain hundreds of seeds. "So, if you get them this year, look at all the work you're saving yourself for next year," says Weedman.

Dame's rocket is another invasive, even though it has an attractive pink-and-white blossom. Some of the students say they've seen this in their own yards. Dame's rocket may look pretty, Weedman explains, but it can destroy the wood-

Learning to identify dame's rocket, a woodland invasive.

lands. "If you see a plant with four petals like this, that's dame's rocket. 'Four no more.' If you find a plant that looks like it but has five petals, don't pick it. 'Five stay alive.'"

The goal today is to grab each invasive near its base so that the entire root comes out. If they find one that's too tough to yank, they can signal one of the grown-ups carrying a shovel to help dig it out.

Each child gets to wear gloves. They're working in cooperative groups of three or four with one bag. Because this important mission will take them completely "off-road" and they can explore anywhere, they seem fired up. They're helping save the woods.

"And remember, when you think your bag is full, put more in it," Weedman says. "It's probably not as full as you think. And remember to be careful of new, native plants that have small white flags. Are you ready, Weed Warriors?"

"Yes!" they shout.

Fairly quickly, the children learn how to spot garlic mustard and dame's rocket as they pull more and more with all their might. As the bags grow heavier, their confidence increases.

"I'm already really good at this 'cuz I used to pull out weeds with my grandma," says one of the girls. "That's how I picked out that big garlic mustard." She waves

the long root. The plant is nearly as tall as she is.

This job seems to encourage co-operation but also storytelling.

When they come upon a large hole, a team takes turns peering inside. "Anybody know what badger tracks look like?" a boy asks.

"Badgers are really mean," another warns. "They'll bite you."

There are shrieks of joy nearby. Several of the boys have figured out that if they use both hands, picking

Mysterious burrow discovery—anyone home?

with the right, then with the left, they can work very quickly stuffing the bag. "Look how much we got! Oh, this is good."

"It's so fun, see? I know a really good way to do it. Oh, that's because I'm older than everybody in my class."

As they push deeper into the woods, some worry they'll meet a wild animal. They hoist their bags over their shoulders and enter deeper into what seems like wilderness. "I don't think you can get lost in there," a girl says.

"If there are snakes, there's a very low chance they're poisonous, right? Probably they're just garter snakes."

The girl refuses to budge. Another girl pushes past her. "Guys, show me the snakes! I want to see snakes."

The fourth graders are among the first to notice that hiding on the edge of the woods are fragrant white blossoms and the first wild raspberries—still green. "Not ripe yet," says a boy. "I'm going to come back when they're ready."

They hurry in teams into a new area of the woods. The garlic mustard roots are sometimes tough to yank. "Oh, look, I have a double one. That's good luck."

Suddenly, a girl calls in a loud voice, "We found a big, fat toad! Look!"

Everyone crowds around her, admiring its size and brown color. The toad holds perfectly still. Another classmate has found its smaller cousin, half its size. "I got another one," he says. "A baby. I never found one before. My first toad."

"I love frogs. And toads."

"Let me hold it, please."

She shows how to gently cup her hands so the toad won't jump away or be squashed. "You can see its heart beating."

When it's time to go, they find a place to release the toad where it won't be stepped on.

Visiting toad calmly pauses to inspect excited students.

"Follow me!" commands a boy who pushes aside the brambles and branches. "Watch out. I'm clearing out some more paths to get the garlic mustard."

When each group returns to the amphitheater, they all receive stickers that say "Weed Warrior."

By mid-afternoon, the woods have become hot and humid. Yet there's lots of jostling and galloping as the fifth graders rush down the trail. "Garlic mustard, peeew! What a stink," a boy complains. "I can see why no animal eats this."

"Oh, my gosh, there's even more! Keep going," the tallest girl says.

The first graders are excited to carry the bags and wear gloves. When they push inside the woods, a few seem nervous. "Are we lost?" one asks.

"The teacher knows the way."

"Let's go down here. Oh, there's a humongous forest of them over here. Deeper in the forest. Oh, come on, guys. What are you waiting for?"

A second grader seems to be intently listening to something near the patch of garlic mustard. He pulls out a plant. "They make a squeaking noise when they come out of the ground. Hear it? Sounds like *eeeeek*."

Thanks to their hard work, the Eagle Nature Trail Team of 181 students and volunteers from the community wins the 2021 Garlic Mustard Pull-A-Thon, an annual fundraising event involving groups from across the area. Over the past eight competitions, the team has pulled a whopping 12,277 pounds of garlic mustard and other invasives. The Eagle Nature Trail Team's name will be added to the traveling Pull-A-Thon trophy from the Southeastern Wisconsin Invasive Species Consortium. (The Eagle Nature Trail team appeared on the trophy plaque as the 2019 winner as well.) With their record-breaking effort in 2021, the Eagle team raised $3,250 in pledged donations, half of which goes to help fund trail projects.

NURTURING NATIVE PLANTS

Tomorrow school is out for the year, but today is warm and the sun shines. There's a sense of urgency as the classes arrive. They're eager to get their hands muddy digging holes and transplanting and watering new plants in the prairie and woodland and along the pond.

Before they begin, the students are encouraged to think about what native plants are and what they do. "Native plants are beautiful," Weedman says. "Butterflies lay eggs on native plants, not roses." Native plants go through cycles, she explains. Even when they look dead in winter, they put all their energy underground and come back in the spring. Bees pollinate flowers. Native plants are helpful to bees and butterflies. And birds can feed on these plants all winter. Butterflies and hummingbirds drink plant nectar. They change with the seasons.

New native plants require care, patience, and teamwork.

Empty jugs brought from home become important water patrol tools.

"Native plants have been around for thousands of years," she says. "They require very little care because they take care of themselves."

Three boys on a team have named their three-stemmed plant Golden Alexander, for "Golden," "Alex," and "Zanders." That way they all have an equal connection to what they're doing as they take turns with the garden trowel.

"Is it ready?"

"No, the hole has to be deeper."

"Use some muscle."

"We got to save him. Save Zanders!"

"I'm going to plant this little guy."

"We might find treasure. That would be cool."

Once the plant has been carefully squeezed from the small plastic pot, it is placed in the hole and dirt is scooped around it. A small white flag nearby warns: "Watch out. New plant."

A team carrying heavy gallon milk jugs filled with water shuffle among the planters, stopping every now and again to carefully tip the jugs and dribble water on the new plants.

"Water? Anyone need water?"

"Over here! Hey, you watered my foot."

"Don't step on the spider. This is his home."

"I found a worm!"

"I don't like spiders, but don't kill them. They're helpful, right?"

"Worms are good luck. Put it in the hole. It makes the soil better."

Everyone is hot and muddy, yet no one complains. This has been a good day to make a difference. The fourth graders look around at the small white flags in the prairie, the woodland, and along the wetland. When one of the boys is asked if he'd like to be a farmer when he grows up, he replies, "No, I want to be a race car driver."

SUMMER WATERING PATROLS

Students in second through fourth grades in this year's summer school class have a big job. Little rain has fallen. As the temperatures rise, the new plants need help staying alive. Each of the students has brought from home an empty milk jug to fill with water. Every morning, a watering patrol sets off down the Eagle Nature Trail with a wagon loaded with heavy jugs. One by one the jugs are emptied into a long-necked watering can. They take turns carefully sprinkling the tender plants in the prairie, woodland, and wetland near the pond.

This morning the prairie is fragrant with sweet milkweed blossoms. Bees hover and sip the nectar. So do white cabbage butterflies and great spangled fritillary butterflies with their orange and black markings. Black and metallic silver spots on these elegant great spangled fritillary butterflies' wings serve as camouflage when they're resting on a blossom or a branch.

Many of the great spangled fritillaries on the prairie this morning may have had their beginnings in the woodland as caterpillars on the wild violets that bloomed earlier, in spring. Later, in summer, the mature female butterfly will lay more than 2,000 eggs in patches of violets. Even though the purple blossoms have wilted and blown away, fritillaries seem to be able to sense where the plants are. Nobody's sure how. Some scientists think the butterflies may smell the violets' roots. The caterpillars will hatch in the fall and immediately find a safe place on the violet plant to sleep through the winter. In the spring, when the violets begin to bloom, the hungry caterpillars wake up and begin to eat.

Sweet milkweed blossoms attract great spangled fritillaries.

By the time the children see great spangled fritillaries in the prairie, the butterflies have already gone on many adventures and managed to stay alive. Now as adult butterflies, they feed on the sweet nectar of many prairie flowers: milkweed blooms, joe-pye weed, wild raspberry blossoms. The butterflies—just like the bees, wasps, and beetles—are helping to pollinate the prairie blooms so that there will be more plants in the spring.

The children work in teams to dribble water on the plants. Each oak tree gets its own gallon jug of water poured at the base where the roots are. A satisfying *glug-glug*!

While the teacher has told them "Don't bug bugs and they won't bug you," there is still much discussion about the many insects big and small they notice as they work.

"Can you see a bumblebee over there?" one of the girls in a fourth-grade trio asks.

"Oh, nononono," her friend says fearfully.

The third girl replies, "A bumble does not sting unless you try to kill it."

"Yeah, leave them alone and they won't hurt you."

"Unless they bump into you."

"That's a fact. They won't hurt you if you're just standing looking at them. I mean, they're just gathering pollen."

The children pull the wagon down the boardwalk toward the pond. The wheels make a noisy *calump-calump* sound. Even if it rains today, watering the new wetland plants is still a good idea. The young plants need all the help they can get.

Even though the pond's water is gone, dragonfly and damselfly larvae hunt insects in the grass that quickly spreads over the pond area. Green frogs and young bullfrogs leap from the woodland to hunt insects among the green growth. The pond may be empty of water, but there's still a lot of life here.

"I miss the pond," says a boy sadly as he looks out from the boardwalk. When he's told that the pond will be back next year with snowmelt and spring rains, he replies, "I can't wait until then."

A group of girls discover that the wild raspberries are finally ripe. They begin to pick and taste the purple fruit. "The smell reminds me of green apples," one says.

"I love the baby berries. The baby ones are so juicy. They're really good."

One girl sticks out her purple tongue and shows her purple hands.

As the watering brigade loads their supplies into the wagon, the children pause to inspect anthills. A troop of ants wander along the dry ground in single file, following a trace of chemical scent that creates a kind of path on the Eagle Nature Trail.

A boy crouches on the ground to watch the field ants carrying bits of what look like seeds back to their nest, a hole in the ground on the edge of the prairie. "These ants are just saying hi to their neighbors, see? They're just walking around."

"Ants are very busy," another boy agrees. "They love having playdates."

The children seem surprised to learn that ants can move more soil than earthworms. Ants help aerate the soil with the holes they make, cycle nutrients, and move seeds to new locations. For something so small, they do a lot of important cooperative work to help keep the prairie healthy.

"You don't have to be afraid of ants," one of the fourth-grade girls says. "They're just like us."

BIBLIOGRAPHY

Bergland, Martha and Paul G. Hayes. *Studying Wisconsin: The Life of Increase Lapham.* Madison: Wisconsin Historical Society Press, 2014.

Berry, Wendell. *The Unsettling of America: Culture and Agriculture.* San Francisco: Sierra Club Books, 1996.

Brockman, Kay M. and Richard A. Dow Jr. *Wildlife in Early Wisconsin: A Collection of Works by A.W. Schorger.* Stevens Point, WI: Student Chapter of the Wildlife Society, 1982.

Brown, Lauren and Ted Elliman. *Grasses, Sedges, Rushes.* New Haven, CT: Yale University Press, 2020.

Childs, Craig. *Atlas of a Lost World: Travels in Ice Age America.* NY: Pantheon, 2018.

Clayton, Lee. *Pleistocene Geology of Waukesha County, WI.* Wisconsin Geological and Natural History Survey, Bull. 99, 2001.

Cochrane, Theodore S. *Atlas of Wisconsin Prairie and Savanna Flora.* Tech. Bulletin No. 191, Wisconsin Department of Natural Resources, 2000.

Current, Richard N. *The History of Wisconsin, Vol. I, Vol. II.* Madison, WI: State Historical Society of Wisconsin, 1976.

Curtis, John T. *The Vegetation of Wisconsin.* Madison: University of Wisconsin Press, 1959.

Daniels, Jaret C. *Vibrant Butterflies.* Cambridge, MN: Adventure Publications, 2018.

Heinrich, Bernd. *Winter World: The Ingenuity of Animal Survival.* NY: HarperCollins, 2003.

Helzer, Chris. *Hidden Prairie Photographing Life in One Square Meter.* Iowa City: University of Iowa Press, 2020.

Langill, Ellen D. and Jean Penn Loerke, ed. *From Farmland to Freeways: A History of Waukesha County, Wisconsin.* Waukesha, WI: Waukesha County Historical Society, 1984.

Leopold, Aldo. "Land Ethic," Essay from *Sand County Almanac.* NY: Oxford University Press, 1949.

Loew, Patty. *Indian Nations of Wisconsin.* Madison: Wisconsin Historical Society Press, 2nd Edition, 2013.

Lorenzsonn, Axel. *Steam & Cinders: The Advent of Railroads in Wisconsin.* Madison: Wisconsin Historical Society Press, 2009.

Madson, John. *Where the Sky Began: Land of the Tallgrass Prairie.* Boston: Houghton Mifflin, 1982.

Mirk, Walter. *Tallgrass Prairie of the Upper Midwest.* The Prairie Enthusiasts Publication, 1987.

Moor, Robert. *On Trails: An Exploration.* NY: Simon & Schuster, 2016.

Olsson, Nils William, ed. *A Pioneer in Northwest America, 1841–1858, The Memoirs of Gustaf Unonius, Vol. II.* Minneapolis: University of Minnesota Press, 1960.

Ostergren, Robert C., ed. *Wisconsin Land and Life.* Madison: University of Wisconsin Press, 1997.

Pielou, E.C. *After the Ice Age: The Return of Life to Glaciated North America.* Chicago: University of Chicago Press, 1991.

Sayre, Robert F., ed. *Recovering the Prairie.* Madison: University of Wisconsin Press, 1999.

Stevens, William K. *Miracle Under the Oaks: The Revival of Nature in America.* NY: Pocket Books, Simon & Schuster, 1995.

Tallamy, Douglas W. *The Nature of Oaks.* Portland, OR: Timber Press, 2021.

Tekiela, Stan. *Majestic Eagles.* Cambridge, MN: Adventure Publications, 2007.

Tekiela, Stan. *Reptiles and Amphibians of Wisconsin Field Guide.* Cambridge, MN: Adventure Publications, 2004.

Wechsler, Doug. *Frog Heaven: Ecology of a Vernal Pool.* Honesdale, PA: Boyds Mill Press, 2006.

Wisconsin Cartographers' Guild. *Wisconsin's Past and Present: A Historical Atlas.* Madison: University of Wisconsin Press, 1998.

Southeastern Wisconsin, History of Old Milwaukee County, Vol. I. Chicago: SJ Clarke Publishing Co., 1932.

Wyman, Mark. *The Wisconsin Frontier.* Bloomington, IN: Indiana University Press, 1998.

ARTICLES

Dorney, John R., "The Impact of Native Americans on Presettlement Vegetation in Southeastern Wisconsin," Transactions of Wisconsin Academy of Sciences, Arts and Letters, Vol. 69, 1981. Pages 26–36.

Goc, Michael J., "The Wisconsin Dust Bowl," The Magazine of History, Spring 1990, Vol. 73, No. 3 (Spring, 1990), pp. 162–201.

Kent, Mara, "Wood v. Boynton and the Incredible Journey of the Eagle Diamond," Wisconsin Magazine of History, Winter 2013–14, pp. 44–53.

"Land Survey Information," Board of Commissioners of Public Lands, https://digicoll.library.wisc.edu/SurveyNotes/SurveyInfo.html.

Prell, Renae, "A History and Survey of Historical Vegetation Mapping in Wisconsin," Wisconsin Geographer, 1989 (Vol. 5), pp. 60–68.

Sasso, Robert F. and Dan Joyce, "Ethnohistory and Archaeology: The Removal Era Potawatomi Lifeway in Southeastern Wisconsin," Midcontinental Journal of Archaeology, Spring 2006, Vol. 31, No. 1 (Spring 2006), pp. 165–201.

Wilson, Trelen, "Plant Species Inventory and Evaluation of Some Prairie Remnants in Waukesha, County, WI," Fifth Midwest Prairie Conference Proceedings: Ames, IO, Iowa State University, Aug. 22–24, 1976, pp. 39–45.

Wisconsin Public Land Survey Records: Original Field Notes and Plat Maps, Waukesha County, Wisconsin Board of Commissioners of Public Lands, published by US General Land Office. http://images.library.wisc.edu/imageConversion/EFacs4.img?collection.

MAPS

Whitford, Philip and Peter Salamun, "Map of Milwaukee County Showing the Original Vegetation as Taken from Land Survey Records of 1835–1836," in "An Upland Forest Survey of the Milwaukee Area," Ecology, Vol. 35, 1954.

"Wisconsin Land Economic Inventory," Town of Eagle, c. 1933–1945, Wisconsin Department of Agriculture, Bordner Survey, University of Wisconsin, Madison, Library. https://search.library.wisc.edu/digital/A2NLLOSZDZPAM59B.

"Early Vegetation of Wisconsin," Geological and Natural History Survey, University of Wisconsin, Extension, Cottam, G. Loucks, O.L. Curtis, J.T., Series number M035, 1965. https://wgnhs.wisc.edu/catalog/publication/000360/resource/m035.

"Presettlement Vegetation of Waukesha County, 1836," map by Johnson, Marlin, and Schwartzmeir, Jerry, p. 23, From Farms to Freeways.

"Map of the County of Waukesha, Wisconsin: from surveys under the direction of H.F. Walling, published by M. H. Tyler, 1859. https://collections.lib.uwm.edu/digital collection/agdm/id/103.

"Eagle Township Mill Pond, Waukesha County, 1873," Published by Harrison and Warner, 1873.

"Plat book of Waukesha County, Wisconsin, drawn from actual surveys and the county records by C.M. Foote & J.W. Henion," 1849–1899; Minneapolis, MN: C.M. Foote & Col, 1891.

"Plat book of Waukesha County Wisconsin, Eagle," W.W. Hixson & Col, 1922.

"Sketch Map, Township 5 North Range 17 E," Board of Commissioners of Public Lands, UW–Madison Libraries. https://digcoll.library.wisc.edu/cgi-bin/WureyNotes/SurveyNotes-id.

"Map of Waukesha County, Wis." Published by the Waukesha Weekly Press, 1900. https://cdm15932.contentdm.oclc.org/digital/collection/maps/id/1815.

Map of Section 23, Eagle Township, Waukesha County, 1835, from survey notes by Mullett & Brink, August 17, 1835, Robert Clark Jr., certified, Jan. 19, 1836, published by U.S. General Surveyors Office. http://images.library.wisc.edu/imageConversion/EFacs4.img?collection.

AERIAL MAPS

1956, 1966, 1969, 1979, 1992 USDA Aerial Maps from Map & Geospatial Data Librarian Arthur H. Robinson Map Library, Department of Geography, University of Wisconsin–Madison. https://uwmadison.box.com/s/f3br1cybhb6yestz6vu7yiea4rkz4rin.

Waukesha County, 1937, UWDC, UW–Madison Libraries.
https://search.library.wisc.edu/digital/ANS3CMP-PKRGEXY8X/Full.
1941 Waukesha County GIS MAP.
2020 Waukesha County GIS Map.

MANUSCRIPTS

Griffin Family letters, 1842–1876, Wisconsin Historical Society, Special Collections.
Increase Lapham Papers, Boxes 12, 13, 14, 15, 16, 20, 22, Wisconsin Historical Society, Special Collections.

SOURCE NOTES

Page v "Nature is . . . for it." Interview by author with Beth Dobberstein, March 2020.

Page v "When we . . . respect." Leopold, Aldo. *Sand County Almanac*. NY: Simon & Schuster, 1949.

Page 2 "If the board . . . anything." Interview by author with Dave Traver, March 2021.

Page 3 "Nobody . . . that." Interview by author with Jean Weedman, December 22, 2020.

Page 3 "a dead zone" Interview by author with Jerry Ziegler, email correspondence, July 12, 2021.

Page 4 "That noise . . . surprise." Interview by author with Jean Weedman, email correspondence, July 24, 2021.

Page 4 "Frogs . . . wetland," Interview by author with Jerry Ziegler, email correspondence, July 12, 2021.

Page 5 "There's . . . humans." Ibid.

Page 5 "to create . . . adults." Interview with Jean Weedman, March 2020.

Page 5 "You have . . . need," "Everyone . . . . a relationship." Interview with Dave Traver, March 2021.

Pages 5–6 "You start . . . . effort." Ibid.

Page 6 "They may . . . offer." Ibid.

Page 8 "leaping and jumping," "Some . . . library!" Interview by author with Maria Hinners, May 25, 2021.

Page 9 "You see . . . . screen." Interview by author with Matt Stich, March 2020.

Page 9 "Sometimes . . . . change." Interview by author with Jean Weedman, December 22, 2020; March 2020.

Page 14 "shatter zone" p. 24–5, Wyman, Mark. *The Wisconsin Frontier*. Bloomington, IN: Indiana University Press, 1998.

Pages 16–17 "Treaty after . . . homelands." p. 105, Loew, Patty. *Indian Nations of Wisconsin*. Madison: Wisconsin Historical Society Press, 2nd Edition, 2013.

Page 23 "land moderately . . . prairie." "Land west . . . rate." "Land Survey Information," Board of Commissioners of Public Lands, https://digicoll.library.wisc.edu/SurveyNotes/SurveyInfo.html; Wisconsin Public Land Survey Records: Original Field Notes and Plat Maps, Waukesha County, Wisconsin Board of Commissioners of Public Lands, published by US General Land Office. http://images.library.wisc.edu/imageConversion/EFacs4.img?collection.

Page 23 "stands . . . oak." Ibid.

Page 23 "wet prairie . . . . stakes. " Ibid.

Page 24 "Indian trails." Map of Section 23, Eagle Township, Waukesha County, 1835, from survey notes by Mullett & Brink, August 17, 1835, Robert Clark Jr., certified, Jan. 19, 1836, published by U.S. General Surveyors Office. http://images.library.wisc.edu/imageConversion/EFacs4.img?collection.

Page 26 "The fire . . . . flames." p. 29, Langill, Ellen D. and Jean Penn Loerke, ed. *From Farmland to Freeways: A History of Waukesha County, Wisconsin*. Waukesha, WI: Waukesha County Historical Society, 1984.

Page 26 "The Prairie Farm" Waukesha County Estate Proceedings, Court Record, November 3, 1894.

Page 26 "The Prairie . . . . to me." p. 169, Sayre, Robert F., ed. *Recovering the Prairie*. Madison: University of Wisconsin Press, 1999.

Page 27 "like . . . sky." p. 159, Muir, John. *The Story of My Boyhood and Youth*. Mineola, NY: Dover Publications, 2018.

Page 27 "We plowed . . . undoing." Berry, Wendell. *The Unsettling of America: Culture and Agriculture*. San Francisco: Sierra Club Books, 1996.

Page 30 Information about the dust storms of 1934 P. 1736, Goc, Michael J. "The Wisconsin Dust Bowl," *The Magazine of History*, Spring, 1990, Vol. 73, No. 3 (Spring, 1990) pp. 162-201.

Page 31 "You should . . . snow." Ibid.

Page 31 "the current . . . . use." "Wisconsin Land Economic Inventory," Town of Eagle, c. 1933–45, Wisconsin Department of Agriculture, Bordner Survey, University of Wisconsin, Madison, Library. https://search.library.wisc.edu/digital/A2NLLOSZDZPAM59B.

Page 33 Information about Frank Splechter and family: Interview by author with Splechter relative, Barbara Ziemer, Sept. 3, 2021.

Page 34 Information about the value of the condition and value of Splechter holding: Federal Census Record, 1940.

Pages 34–35 Information about Agnes Splechter: Interviews by author with B. Ziemer, Aug. 22, 2021 & Sept. 3, 2021.

Pages 34–35 Information about Fritzy Splechter's enlistment and service in the Army: U.S. World War II Draft Card, Frances Splechter https://www.ancestry.com/discoveryuicontent/view/199065890:2238?tid=&pid=&queryId=59320dc05a5b5edea3e137e59e2ca861&_phsrc=jzC276&_phstart=successSource; Interview with B. Ziemer, August 22, 2021.

Page 35 Information about Agnes Splechter's purchase of Splechter land: Waukesha Deed Records, Eagle Township, NW Quarter Section 23 T5Range 17E. 1940-45, page. 50.

Page 35 Information about Fritzy Splechter's death: Interviews by author with B. Ziemer, August 22, 2021 & Sept. 3, 2021; "The Battle of the Huertgen Forest: After Action Report 60th Infantry Regiment, for the period of 1 Oct.–17 Oct. 1944." http://home.scarlet.be/-sh446368/aar-60th-inf-oct-2.html; "Obituary," Waukesha Daily Freeman, Waukesha, WI, Monday, November 17, 1947, p. 2, Col. 5.; National Archives and Records Administration, U.S. World War II Hospital Admission Card File (1942-1954), Frances T. Splechter, October 1944. https://search.ancestry.com/cgi-bin/sse.dll?dbid=61817&h=16853034&indiv=try&o_vc=Record:OtherRecord&rhSource=2238.

Page 36 "She was . . . person." Interview by author with B. Ziemer, August 22, 2021.

Page 36 Information about the sale of Splechter land to the Wisconsin Conservation Department: "Plan Rites for Eagle Veteran," Waukesha Daily Freeman, November 17, 1947. P. 2. Waukesha County, Eagle Township, Deeds, March 26, 1965. Harrington, C.L., "Story of Kettle Moraine State Forest," The Wisconsin Magazine of History, Spring 1954, Vol. 37, No. 3 (Spring 1954) pp. 143–5.

Page 37 "Fritzy . . . . pleased." Interview with B. Ziemer, Aug. 22, 2021.

Page 39 "This is our nature trail," "Just follow me." Sept. 10, 2021, Transcription of morning on trail, first through fifth grades.

Page 40 "Trees . . . .time." Ibid.

Page 40 "So small!" "See how . . . grew?" Ibid.

Page 41 "Watch . . . . our family." Ibid.

Page 43 "It's a . . . time." Interview with Maria Hinners, Jan. 5, 2020.

Page 43 "A pine!" Transcript of visit to trail, third grade, Sept. 24, 2021.

Page 43 "Mine . . . it." Ibid.

Page 43 "I sit . . . rains." Ibid.

Page 43 "My favorite . . . tree." Ibid.

Page 43 "I don't . . . called." Ibid.

Page 44 "This way!" Ibid.

Page 44 "Look up!" Ibid.

Page 44 "Just like . . . read!" Ibid.

Page 44 "very . . . chips." Ibid.

Page 45 "So . . . . home." Ibid.

Page 45 "It's a . . . trail." Interview, Alli Chase, Sept. 24, 2021.

Page 47 "The firest . . . me." Interview with Maria Hinners, Jan. 5, 2020.

Page 48 "The trail . . . . way." Interview with Matt Stich, March 2020.

Page 48 "There's . . . . hope." Interview with Beth Dobberstein, March 2020.

Page 49 "The main . . . . backyard." Interview with Tammy Mueller, Jan. 11, 2021.

Pages 50–51 Marlin Jonson Johnson's list of cold-weather-friendly activities and science experiments: Interview with Marlin Jonson Johnson, July 19, 2021.

Page 54 "Watch . . . out." Transcription of April 30, 2021, on trail with third grade.

Page 54 "See . . . bloom." Ibid.

Page 54 "Look . . . . fox." Ibid.

Page 54 "And excited." Ibid.

Page 54 "The fresh . . . . indoors." Ibid.

Page 56 "If we . . . . again." Transcription of May 24, visit on trail with first grade.

Page 56 "Pick up trash." Ibid.

Page 56 "Recycle . . . ground." Ibid.

Page 56 "Plant trees." Ibid.

Page 56 "Water plants." Ibid.

Page 56 "If you . . . back." Ibid.

Page 57 "I found . . . house!" Transcription of April 22, 2021, visit on trail with third grade.

Page 57 "Bones . . . . bones." Ibid.

Page 58 "Happy Earth Day!" Ibid.

Page 58 "Drawing . . . . again." Transcription of May 20, 2021, visit on trail with second and third grade combined class.

Page 58 "I listen . . . . ideas." Ibid.

Page 60 "Clearly . . . . rabbits." Interview with Matt Wilhelm, May 6, 2021.

Page 61 "Takes . . . together." May 6, 2021 Zoom presentation by Matt Wilhelm.

Page 61 "This was . . . helped." Interview with Matt Wilhelm, May 6, 2021.

Page 64 "taking turns," P. 8, Mirk, Walter. Tallgrass Prairie of the Upper Midwest. The Prairie Enthusiasts Publication, 1987.

Page 65 "Like garlic pizza," Transcription of all-school invasive weed pulling, June 2, 2021.

Page 65 "So, if . . . year." Ibid.

Page 66 "If you . . . . alive." Ibid.

Page 66 "And remember . . . . Warriors?" Ibid.

Page 66 "Yes!" Ibid.

Page 66 "I'm . . . . mustard." Ibid.

Page 67 "Anybody . . . like?" Ibid.

Page 67 "Badgers . . . . you." Ibid.

Page 67 "It's . . . . class." Ibid.

Page 67 "I don't . . . there," Ibid.

Page 67 "If there . . . . snakes." Ibid.

Page 67 "Guys . . .snakes." Ibid.

Page 67 "Not . . . ready." Ibid.

Page 67 "Oh, look . . . . luck." Ibid.

Page 67 "We . . . . Look!" Ibid.

Page 68 "I got . . . . toad." Ibid.

Page 68 " I love . . . . toads." Ibid.

Page 68 "Let . . . please." Ibid.

Page 68 "You . . beating." Ibid.

Page 68 "Follow . . . . mustard." Ibid.

Page 68 "Weed Warrior!" Ibid.

Page 68 "Garlic . . . . this." Ibid.

Page 68 "Oh, my . . . . going," Ibid.

Page 68 "Are we lost?" Ibid.

Page 68 "The teacher . . . way?" Ibid.

Page 69 "Let's . . . . for?" Ibid.

Page 69 "They . . . . eeek." Ibid.

Page 69 "Native . . . . roses." Transcription of planting of native plants, third grade, June 1, 2021.

Pages 69–70 "Native . . . . themselves." Ibid.

Page 70 "Is it ready?" Ibid.

Page 70 "No . . . deeper." Ibid.

Page 70 "Use some muscle." Ibid.

Page 70 "We got . . . . Zanders!" Ibid.

Page 70 "I'm . . . guy." Ibid.

Page 70 "We . . . . cool." Ibid.

Page 70 "Watch . . . . plant." Ibid.

Page 70 "Water . . . . water?" Ibid.

Page 70 "Over . . . . foot." Ibid.

Page 70 "Don't . . . . home." Ibid.

Page 70 "I found a worm!" Ibid.

Page 70 "I don't . . . . right?" Ibid.

Page 70 "Worms . . . . better." Ibid.

Page 71 "No . . . diver." Ibid.

Page 72 "Don't bug . . . you," Transcription of multi-grade summer school class, June 24, 2021.

Page 73 "Can . . . there?" Ibid.

Page 73 "Oh, nonononono," Ibid.

Page 73 "Yeah . . . you." Ibid.

Page 73 "Unless . . . you." Ibid.

Page 73 "That's . . . . pollen." Ibid.

Page 73 "I miss . . . then." Ibid.

Page 73 "The smell . . . apples," Ibid.

Page 73 "I love . . . good." Ibid.

Page 74 "These . . . . around." Ibid.

Page 74 "Ants . . . . playdates." Ibid.

Page 74 "You don't . . . . us." Ibid.

ACKNOWLEDGMENTS

Writing a book is a lot like a long hike in the woods. You never know what you'll encounter along the way. I feel fortunate to have had so many generous fellow travelers and environmental enthusiasts to point out essential discoveries and keep me on track when I was feeling lost. Their enthusiasm and knowledge helped make this a wondrous journey.

Jean Weedman, extraordinary trail founder, organizer, and environmental educator, has been an essential guide. She and her husband, Tom, have inspired ongoing stewardship with a great group of volunteers, including Karen Akroff, Nancy Wilhelm, Irene Roberts, Mark Schoesson, and many others. This book would not have been possible without the photographic talents of Dawn-Marie Staccia, another key trail volunteer. Dave Traver, one of the original trail founders, provided essential interviews. Jerry Ziegler generously provided historical and environmental observations.

Over the course of more than a year—in different seasons and weathers—I was privileged to witness and take part in visits to the Eagle Nature Trail with students from pre-K through fifth grade at Eagle Elementary. Their energy and candid observations inspired me. Special thanks go to amazing teachers who saw the benefits of getting outdoors with their classes—especially during the challenging months of COVID-19: Tammy Mueller, Beth Dobberstein, Amy Muth, Courtney Helm, and many others. Matt Stich, former principal, provided invaluable insights about kids and nature. Alli Chase, director of Alice Baker Memorial Library, and Maria Hinners, former youth services librarian, were essential in sharing details about the trail-school alliance.

My trek took me to many libraries and archives staffed with helpful individuals, including Henry Hecker of the Mukwonago Historical Society, John Schoenknecht of the Waukesha County Historical Society, volunteers at the Eagle Historical Society, and a team of top-notch reference librarians at Oconomowoc Public Library. Lee Grady, reference archivist, Wisconsin Historical Society, revealed hidden resources about Increase Lapham. Lisa Marine, Image Reproduction, Wisconsin Historical Society, provided key photo help. Jamie Martindale, Map & Geospatial Data Librarian, Arthur H. Robinson Map Library, Department of Geography, University of Wisconsin-Madison, unscrambled how to understand aerial photography.

Jim Jackley provided remarkable help with title and deed searches. Marlin Johnson was key in explaining the workings of early surveys and pre-settlement vegetation maps. Dan Carter, Landowner Services Coordinator, Prairie Enthusiasts, identified the sole surviving Eagle Prairie remnant. Jesse Steinke shared amazing early family photos in the area. Barb Ziemer, a surprise along the way, was an amazing resource regarding her great-aunt Agnes, who was one of the heroes of the Eagle Nature Trail story.

This book would not have been possible without the vision and energy of my editor, Mary Cash, whose enthusiasm and skill pushed forward this remarkable and timely series, Books for a Better Earth. My appreciation also goes to my family, whose support has been a boundless gift. Throughout this book's journey, I was inspired by the marvelous company of tireless hikers Keira and Vivian, my granddaughters. And, of course, my husband and lifelong fellow traveler, Jack.

PHOTO CREDITS

Laurie Lawlor: i, vi, 6, 10, 12, 14, 18, 22, 40, 47, 48, 49, 52, 54, 55, 56, 58, 62, 64 (right), 65, 66, 67, 68, 70 (bottom)

Mukwonago Historical Society Museum, Grutzmacher Family Photography Collection: 25 (top), 25 (bottom)

Public Domain: 35 (both)

Isabella Schroepfer: 38

Dawn-Marie Staccia: iv (top), 4 (right), 9, 15, 42, 64 (left), 72

Sprague Photo collection in care of the descendants, the Steinke Family, Courtesy of Jessy Steinke: 25 (middle)

Dave Traver: iv (bottom), 70 (top)

University of Wisconsin-Madison Libraries, Digital Map Collection, USDA, Roll exposure 19-1721, scale: (1:20,000): 32

University of Wisconsin-Madison Libraries, Arthur H. Robinson Map Library, Department of Geography, Wisconsin DNR Image, taken 8-30-1992; WKE S063 15 64 (scale 1:15,840): 37

University of Wisconsin-Madison, Wisconsin Geological and Natural History Survey: 20

Jean Weedman: 2, 4 (left), 7 (both), 44

Matthew Wilhelm: 60, 61

Wisconsin Historical Society, Collections Division, from the collection of Alphonse Gerend/Image 64640: 16

INDEX

Page numbers in *italics* refer to illustrations.